D1526625

CRUISING MAIN STREET

Volume One

Tim Sykes

CONTENTS

Photographs and Memorabilia

The images shown in this book are from the collections of the following photographers and collectors:

Bob Jones
Carla Henning
Carrie Drew Smith
Randy Goudeseune
Wayne Huber
Jason Holiff
Cindy Hartman
Vince Gratton
Mark Vasco
Dianne Huggins
Pat Gillies

Michael Swanson
Joy Henning
Hal Tilley
Milt Houle
Gary Dale
Bill Kydd
George Gray
Bob Gellatly
Jim Ryan
Ken Roberts
Tim Cross

Tim Sykes

Piston Pushers Car Club
Motor Lords Car Club
Galt Strokers Car Club
Guelph Museum
McMaster University
Cambridge Archives
Hamilton Vintage Photos
London Free Press
Cambridge Public Library
Warren Grimm
London Auto Modifiers

CRUISING MAIN STREET
The Experience

As a teenager during the 1950's, the idea of driving a car all around town on a warm summer night was the epitome of freedom and expression, an exuberant right of passage, and a dream fulfilled. Could there be anything as exciting? To be seen out on the streets in the coolest car, showing it off in front of the biggest audience in town may have been the most natural high available. There were places to go and people to meet and to do it in a hot rod or custom car was the bomb.

The dazzling glow from neon signs on store fronts and movie theatres drew crowds naturally to the downtown core, attracted to the nightlife and lively activity. Interconnected side streets directed those same people to other attractions as well.

Drive-in restaurants were another place where young people loved to congregate, and every city in Ontario had a variety to choose from. Originally, most were homegrown "mom and pop" locations, offering an excellent menu of freshly prepared dishes and personal service. In the mid-1950's, early franchised names started to become popular in many communities including Kentucky Fried Chicken, Dairy Queen, and especially A&W. They were joined in the late 1950's and early 1960's by other Canadian and American franchises such as Harvey's, Burger Chef, Little Caesars Pizza, Red Barn and many others. Each of these fast food drive-ins became a central hub of car activity and a cruising destination for many young people.

Cruising up and down Main Street was not unique to any certain city or town. This extra curricular activity happened in nearly every community everywhere, as we shall explore in this book series. Whether your Main Street experience was two blocks long, or 10 miles in length, the fun and the thrill was the same.

The pride of vehicular ownership, the need to be together with friends, and the freedom of movement were all key components in why we enjoyed cruising Main Street. This book series explores this unique era in depth, so enjoy the journey.

I'll meet you downtown!

CRUISING MAIN STREET
A Pictorial Introduction

Bumper to bumper cruising along Main Street

Car dealers, always a good place to meet fellow enthusiasts

Another great place to meet other car guys was the gas station

Meeting the guys at the diner to talk cars

Drive-in restaurants brought cars and young people together

A fun and inexpensive place to bring your date.

Hop in the car, come as you are

Friends meet up at the drive-in to eat and check out hot cars

Cozy up with your date at the school dance

Roller skating and bowling were both popular pastime activities

It was also the era of the hot rod and custom car clubs

T. ORONTO
A. REA
C. AR
C. LUBS

PRES. **STAN PRIDE,** 4 LARCHMERE CR.
HUMBER SUMMIT, ONT – 741-7263

VICE-PRES. **DEREK BROWN,** 29 DUFFIELD RD.
WESTON, ONT – 241-6903

SECY. **DAVE McCAFFERY,** 82 DONMORE DR.
NEWMARKET, ONT – 895-2453

TRANSMEN
ROD & CUSTOM CLUB

PRES.	VICE PRES.	SECY.
Fred Seale	Roy Waghorn	Bob Scott

AM. 7-3630
– MAIL –
700 Brimley Rd. Scarboro, Ont.

KNIGHTS CAR CLUB

PRES.
DOUG. CUTLER
RICHMOND HILL
ONT.

R. McCARTHY
9737 BATHURST ST.
MAPLE, ONT.

The Highwaymen
CAR CLUB
KITCHENER, ONTARIO

Safety, Care, Courtesy and Common Sense
our first consideration.

Secretary
Ron Hinschberger
343 Wellington St. N.

President
Jerry Kay
89 Plymouth Rd.

KITCHENER, ONTARIO

RACING CLUB
385 Mornington Avenue
LONDON, ONTARIO

PRES.	VICE-PRES.	SECY.
JIM PROWSE	FRED HARRIS	GLEN LACKIE

EVOLUTIONISTS
– CAR CLUB –
TORONTO

PRES.
MIKE SKREPNEK
585 Kennedy Rd.

SECY.
BETTY GRIMBERGEN
Scarboro

Aristocrats
Rod & Custom
RICHMOND HILL, ONT.
SHOW and GO CLUB

President
Fred Urben
101 May Avenue

Secretary-Treasurer
Jim Pollard
55 Church St.

Road Runners Car Club of Hamilton
ESTABLISHED 1956

Car club courtesy cards and logos

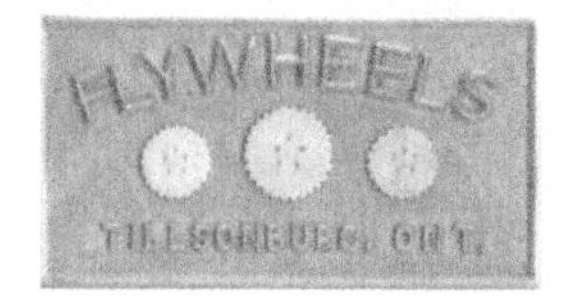

Car club plaques

Car club plaques

HOW TO FORM A HOT ROD CLUB

- PURPOSE
- FOUNDATION
- CONSTITUTION AND BY-LAWS
- ACTIVITIES
- CLUB CHARTERS

NATIONAL HOT ROD ASSOCIATION
1171 NORTH VERMONT
LOS ANGELES 29, CALIF.

DRAG RULES

- SAFETY REGULATIONS
- COMPETITION CLASSES

NATIONAL HOT ROD ASSOCIATION
1171 North Vermont Avenue
Los Angeles 29, California

PRICE 25c

The NHRA was eager to help out fellow enthusiasts

The Drag Strip

Ever heard the phrase? A drag strip is an isolated stretch of pavement where heavy-footed hot-rod drivers can race from dawn to dusk—safely, legally and with a big audience. There are more than 30 such strips scattered across the country, roaring proof that street racing can be taken off the street. Supersouped-up stock cars, motorcycles, homemade cars—anything on wheels—zoom down the strips at speeds up to 130 miles per hour in a race against the clock.

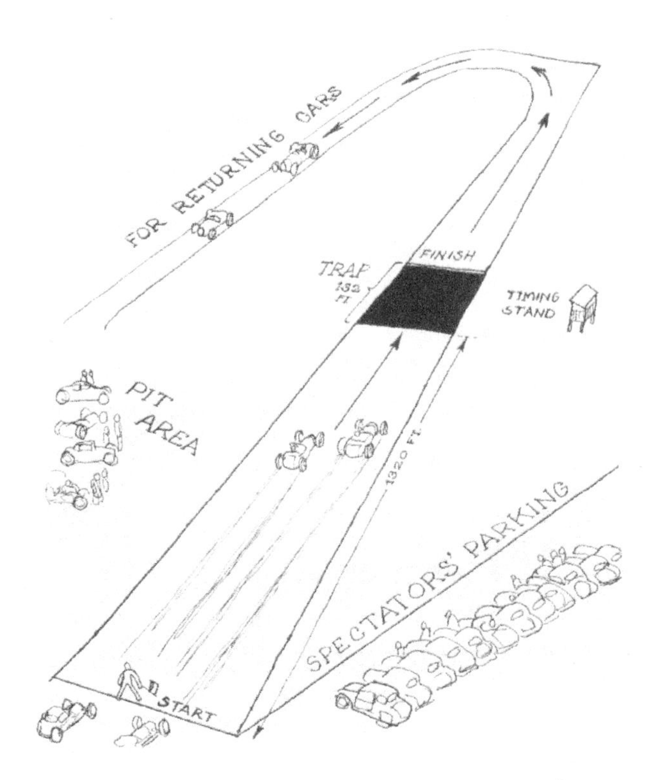

There was a growing interest in going fast

So much to learn each month in the pages of Hot Rod Magazine

'Hot-rods' Increasing Menace to Motorists

TORONTO, May 8. — (CP) — Provincial Police Inspector Albert Witts has expressed alarm over the increasing number of "hot-rods"—cars with souped-up engine power—on Ontario highways.

Testifying before the Ontario Legislature's select committee on highway safety, Inspector Witts said youngsters "have taken over the hot-rod" and are a menace to the motoring public.

"The car of today is a vehicle with power under the hood. Manufacturers, realizing that the people wanted power, has souped up the engines and now the youngsters have taken over" and are increasing power still more to make them into "hot rods".

The temptation for street racing became a problem

1/4 MILE START

John Backe and Cornelius De Jong were fined $25 and costs each by Magistrate W. A. Shaw today when they pleaded guilty to charges of drag racing on Ross St.

Court was told the two were followed at speeds up to 40 miles per hour.

William S. Orbko was fined $25 and costs when he pleaded guilty to speeding at 65 miles per hour in a 40-mile-per-hour zone. Frank James Crandall pleaded guilty to a similar charge and was fined $15 and costs.

Hope New Speed Limit Signs Will Curb Drag Racing

In an effort to halt drag racing on streets bordering the new Vincent Massey Collegiate in Sandwich West the township will erect 25-mile-an-hour speed limit signs.

This action has been prompted after the council received protests from residents in the area surrounding the school, claiming that students driving cars are using the residential streets for drag strips.

In addition to posting of speed curb signs, township police have been instructed to increase its patrol in the district during noon hours and after afternoon dismissal of classes.

Reeve Lawrence Brunet said that Constable Robert Bratt, head of the department's safety division, has been instructed to report to council on effects of this crackdown.

Speedster, Youth Jailed For Month

A Vittoria, Ont., youth was sent to jail for 30 days yesterday as a result of a wild, high-speed chase down Highway 6 last Thursday.

[redacted] 17, pleaded guilty in city magistrate's court to criminal negligence. Police said they chased his car from the intersection of Highways 53 and 6 at speeds up to 105 miles per hour.

[redacted] speeded up when a police cruiser pulled along side him and several times swerved into the lane carrying oncoming traffic. He was finally apprehended when he crashed the car near Caledonia.

"This type of driving has to be stopped," Magistrate Robert Morrison commented. [redacted] licence was suspended for two years.

For decades, the temptation of street racing was always present, however with the influence of organized car clubs and their strict rules, the opening of drag strips as a safe place to race, and the collective knowledge that hot rods are a safe and legitimate form of expression; street racing was thankfully reduced over the years. Showing off by **"cruising the streets"** became the accepted alternative for most car enthusiasts.

CHAPTER ONE
Brantford, Ontario

Throughout the 1950's and 1960's, the city of Brantford was still enjoying a strong economy from several important and successful industrial businesses located within the city limits. Many of Brantford's hard working citizens were employed at large industries such as Massey Harris, Johnson Wax, and Cockshutt Plow.

With a population of about 50,000 during the later part of the 1950's, Brantford's small city charm continued to attract a wide range of residents to the area. Centrally located in the province, the city is less than 60 miles from Toronto, 50 miles from London, and 24 miles from Kitchener.

Throughout the 1950's, the downtown area remained a popular shopping location, as city residents continued to support the local retailers along the main corridors of Colborne and Dalhousie Streets, as well as the many connecting side streets along this key area of the downtown district.

For a teenager growing up in Brantford during this era, this very district became the focus of major cruising activity, especially at night. The bright lights of many of the store fronts seemed to draw crowds of young people eager to experience the excitement, as each neon sign eagerly beckoned patrons into their establishments.

PHIL'S
CAR SALES
USED CARS
BOUGHT – SOLD – TRADED
★ FAIR PRICES, EASY TERMS
752-1920
878 COLBORNE

WEST BRANT
AUTO BODY
GUARANTEED BODY REPAIRS
WE USE SOLDER ON ALL JOBS
Remember: "CHEAP JOB NEVER GOOD
GOOD JOB NEVER CHEAP"
FREE ESTIMATES
753-9752
135 SHERWOOD DR.

FREDDY'S
SERVICE STATION
OPEN 24 HOURS
TOWING
CAA
SUPERTEST
REPAIRS TO ALL
MAKES AND MODELS
756-6612
303 COLBORNE

WEST BRANT
AUTO PAINTERS
JOHN POWESKA PROP.
SPECIALIZED
AUTO REFINISHING
All Work Guaranteed
WEST COLBORNE
SHELLARD LANE
752-4952

LICENSED MECHANIC ON DUTY

Morrell and Burwell Sts. Dial 756-5003

Brantford

A few of Brantford's many auto services available during the 1960's

Piston Pushers, Brantford's historic custom car club is still active

In the 1950's, the variety of good food choices for Brantford youth included The Rhythm Bar Sandwich Shop, an early era burger joint at 75 Colborne Street, known for its delicious food and an excellent selection of early rock and roll records in their jukebox. The Rhythm Bar dance floor was always hopping.

The place to get a great seafood dinner meant a trip to Star Fish and Chips, located at 29 St. George Street.

For a cool treat, everyone ventured to Dairee Delite. Opened in 1953 at the corner of Brant Avenue and Bedford Street, the entire building was moved to its present location at 10 King George Road, back in 1965.

The "new" Loblaw Plaza location of Dairee Delite.

Dairee Delite in 1988. Robbie's "plaza" location beside the bank

Scattered throughout the city were several very popular drive-in restaurants that became the favourite meeting place for these young enthusiasts. Although most of these drive-ins were located along the downtown corridor, there were others that were centered in other locations in town, making for a diverse cruising pattern for hot rod and custom car enthusiasts.

THE FAMILY DRIVE-INS

BRANTFORD
630 Colborne St. E. - 756-5225
Loblaw Plaza, King George Rd. - 756-6175

Michael Swanson's stunning image of Brantford's Shake 'N Burger

SHAKE 'N' BURGER

Restaurant and Drive In

"WHERE GOOD FRIENDS MEET TO EAT"

Robbies Drive-In was located at 630 Colborne St, with a second smaller location in the Loblaw Plaza behind Dairee Delite. A quarter mile away was Shake 'N' Burger, housed within the Mohawk Plaza at 674 Colborne St. Two and half miles further down Colborne was the Pow-Wow Drive-In. These three restaurants became a natural draw for cruising, since they were all located along the main drag in town.

An inside look at the Pow-Wow Drive-In on Colbourne Street

When the A&W Drive-In first opened their doors on the street known as Charing Cross, it immediately became the central hub for cruising in Brantford. This landmark location drew most of the hottest cars in the city, having their parking lot become the place to see and be seen. It also became the most popular starting place for an evening of cruising.

Parking lot photo features intensive cruising at the A&W Drive-In at 67 Charing Cross in Brantford, Ontario. This sensational picture was taken in the summer of 1966 by Michael Swanson.

A & W DRIVE IN
Delicious Food - Fast Car Service
Look for the Bright Orange Building!
A&W ROOT BEER
A&W ROOT BEER

With its downtown streets designated one way only, this situation established a unique cruising circuit for Brantford area car enthusiasts during its peak in the 1960's. During this era, the general circuit was to cruise along the main drag nice and slow, with stops at as many of the local hangouts as possible on any given evening.

After arriving at A&W on Charing Cross, most enthusiasts would hang around for a while, as the parking lot filled up with hot cars. As soon as the sun went down, many of the early arrivals would pull out of the parking lot, turning westbound onto Charing Cross. They would cruise slowly along this street, turning left onto King George Road to travel south. Some would turn into the Loblaw Plaza for a spin through the parking lot in front of the Dairee Delite. After making their presence known, it was time to head downtown. Cruisers would turn left back onto King George and merge onto St. Paul to travel south, and then to turn left onto Brant Avenue and another left onto Colborne Street.

Colborne Street through downtown core would come alive with the sounds of cars and crowds of pedestrians along the sidewalks. Cruising slowly through the downtown streets, your first stop would be Robbies Drive-In at 630 Colborne Street East. It was mandatory to drive slowly through the parking lot to make sure you are seen by everyone. After your appearance was made, it was time to continue your cruise tour, turning right on Colborne Street. Your next destination was located two and a half miles down the road, where the Pow-Wow Drive-In enticed you to stay for the great food.

Whether it was a short or a lengthy visit, a stop at the Pow-Wow was mandatory, as this was the "turn around" for your cruise back through town. When you were ready to continue your evening cruise, a turn right onto Colborne Street had you driving back towards the downtown area. Your next stop had you pull into the Mohawk Plaza for a visit to Shake 'N' Burger. After your stay at "The Shake", another turn right got you back onto Colborne with a merge west onto Dalhousie Street. This stretch of road took you through the heart of Brantford's downtown store fronts and past the landmark Capitol Theatre. After turning right onto Brant Road, St. Paul and King George, the journey had you finally turning right onto Charing Cross to return back to the A&W.

To complete the one way circuit from A&W to the Pow-Wow was approximately 14 miles in length. Just to drive to each stop without purchasing food at any of the destinations, it would take you about 30 minutes to complete this route. If you started at A&W, traveled to Robbies, the Pow-Wow, the "Shake", and then back to A&W, you would be on the road for about an hour. It was a good thing gas prices were cheap back then, but oh what glorious memories we have of this era.

Sadly, each one of these original Brantford cruising destinations is gone today, with the only exception being the Dairee Delite. After more than 65 years in business, this marvelous eatery still opens up each season for a new generation to enjoy.

Shared memories courtesy of the following: Bob Tindale, Terry Freeman, Jeff Fraser, Helen Langille, Edie Mountjoy, Ronald Buttenham, Bob Laking, Henry Poirier, Sharon Wilson Dropko, Jack Curry, Rose MacDonald, Brenda Bridgewater, Terrance Holt, Gloria Crawford, Nancy Waring, Mary Lou Boudreau, Debbie Mummery Beal, Patricia MacArthur, Connie Werkman, Bob Peeling, Don Cornfoot, Carol Gray, Karen Towler, Guy Wilkes, Shirley Wilson, John Last, Larry Walker, Tim Laberge, Larry Smith, John Farrow, Anthony Gambacort, William Kennedy, Gary Berry, Wendy Blair, Les DeHamer, Cathy Cooper, Bill Blower, Dent McIntyre, Barry Kerrigan, Kathryn Bonnie Gleason, Peter Casper Kruger, Ed Jakowetz, Isobel McNair, Sherry Kilcollins de Cuba, Fred M. Johnston, Denise Proulx Methot, Wendy Clement-Ferrell, Larry Morris, Marg Waller Crawford, Bob File, Dorothy Caskenette, James Stuart Cripps, Cindy Allan, Art Savoie, Phil Gillies, Lynn Griggs, Brian Gedney, Tom Peattie, Rick Merrell, Karl Edmison, and other members of the "If you grew up in Brantford" Facebook page.

Special mention goes out to Michael Swanson for his spectacular photo taken at A&W, and his artwork of Brantford's Shake 'N' Burger. Check out his wonderful work at his website: **swansonart.com**

Chapter Two
Cambridge, Ontario

The cruising atmosphere in downtown Galt came alive at night

It might be said that the city of Cambridge, Ontario has experienced a double life. In 1973, the small city of Galt, along with the nearby towns of Preston and Hespeler amalgamated, creating the larger city we know today as Cambridge. However, for most of the older, long time residents of Cambridge, they continue to define themselves as from their older home towns.

Because of this good natured regional defiance, it has made writing this story decidedly more challenging. Light hearted rivalries from decades ago still linger in the hearts and minds of many Cambridge residents.

Regardless, there is a clear picture of the cruising action that did take place within the area during the 1950's and well into the 1960's, and what a history it is. People of this town had a wealth of activity to keep themselves occupied during this era.

Roller skating was an extremely popular activity for many young people throughout the city, with clubs established in all three areas. During the 1960's, roller skaters enjoyed the activity at Galt Arena Gardens on Shade Street, at the Preston Arena on Hamilton Street, as well as the Hespeler Arena on Queen Street.

Galt Arena

The Old Preston Arena

The Old Hespeler Arena

Galt Collegiate Institute, the home of "Teen Town"

Among the many activities for students was the formation of "Teen Town", a student-based organizing committee that hosted youth dances that were held at the YMCA building at Queens Square in the downtown core.

TEEN-TOWN

FOR TEENAGERS:

Providing the best in entertainment for the youth of Galt, and district since 1944.

BY TEENAGERS

EXECUTIVE FOR 1956-57

President—GEORGE PETER
Vice-Pres.—TOM TUMILTY
Treasurer—NORM. HIMES
Secretary—JANE LaROGUE

Teen Town committee at G.C.I.

Teen town dances were very popular and well attended

While attending a Teen Town dance, one of the regular attendees became frustrated, troubled by what he was experiencing during the course of the evening. He had noticed that early on, the disc jockey playing the music began to repeat songs. Confused by the lack of continuity and the disc jockey's sparse musical selection, the young man approached the dance organizer to question why the choice of music was so thin. It seems that the disc jockey that night did not have a lot of experience and only had a very limited selection of songs to play. Nobody at the time could have imagined the change that was about to happen throughout the dance halls across the city. The young man with an amazingly acute awareness for the music of the era was Hal Tilley.

Hal Tilley

Immediately after the dance that night, Tilley approached the dance organizers with a new proposition. With a vast knowledge of various musical styles (particularly doo-wop, rhythm and blues, and early rock and roll), an extensive personal collection of records, and a natural ability to understand what the youth of the day would enjoy, he volunteered to disc jockey at an upcoming dance.

Participants of Hal Tilley's first dance party

Without much initial fanfare, his first dance was an immediate hit, with the dance floor constantly filled for the entire evening.

Another dance was soon planned, which again brought a new level of excitement to these events. Something special was happening, with a level of excitement never before felt anywhere in the city.

Y.W.C.A.
CLUB "40"
HAL TILLEY
and His Records
This Sat. Night
8:30 to 11:30
Dress Shirt and Tie
Ages 15 to 21
ADMISSION 50c

The YWCA was the home of Hal Tilley's popular Club "40" dances

Suddenly, a lot of people were talking about this young disc jockey who completely understood the music everyone wanted to hear and dance to. It wasn't long before nearly every young person in town wanted to attend a dance hosted by "Hal Tilley and his Records". As his reputation grew, it wasn't long that practically every one of his weekends was booked solid.

Hal Tilley was truly a pioneer, bringing rock and roll music to local dances at a level and quality that simply wasn't available anywhere else.

There was an abundance of important hot rod car clubs in town included the Galt Strokers, a group of enthusiasts that were first organized in 1954, and are still active today.

Dependability - Capability

The Galt Strokers

AT YOUR SERVICE ON THE ROAD

"The club that COURTESY built"

DELTA PARK GALT, ONTARIO

Founding member Al Howlett with two of his early hot rods

John Corbett's roadster

Longtime member Bob Drew works on his 1932 Ford roadster

Galt Strokers dragster behind the club house. Club members built this car in Galt and raced at Kohler Drag Strip, back in the 1950's

The Motor Lords Car Club was established in Preston back in 1957 and remains an active club, with an impressive club house located on Pinebush Road.

Motor Lords first club house on Hespeler Road near Log Cabin

Ford coupe belonged to Motor Lords founding member Larry Brain

This primered 1955 Chevrolet was often seen around town

The Tyrods Car Club has been active in Galt since 1963, and still holds organized events for members and friends.

Tyrods member Tim Cross' 1932 Chevy coupe

When the Galt Strokers began limiting their membership, the all new Galt Road Rajahs Car Club was formed.

Galt Road Rajahs first club house

Club crest from the Preston Car Club

The Escorts Car Club was established in Preston in the 1960's, but is no longer active today.

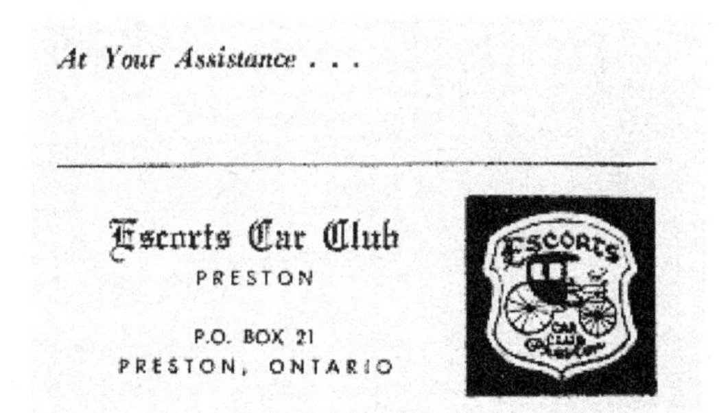

At Your Assistance . . .

Escorts Car Club
PRESTON

P.O. BOX 21
PRESTON, ONTARIO

10 youthful members of the Escorts Car Club of Preston

Galt hot rod history was made in this single garage on Harris Street

McIntyre's Garage on Oxford Street was a popular gathering spot

During the early 1960's, Cambridge had its share of street racing activities which were performed out on newly paved roads located on the outskirts of town where traffic was of little concern back then. Some of these makeshift drag strips included specific lengths of Townline Road, Pinebush Road, Beaverdale Road, Roseville Road and a little-used straightaway along the far side of Puslinch Lake.

Cambridge had more than its share of great diners and drive-in restaurants to frequent during these years. Strategically located in various parts of the city, these fabulous eateries determined the course of many cruising patterns that became the norm for more than a few car crazy youths.

During the early 1950's, there were several downtown Galt diners and restaurants that were popular places worth visiting. Along Water Street, Tops Restaurant and George's were must visits. On Main Street, the diner inside Woolworths was very popular, as was the Diana Restaurant located across the street.

Tops Restaurant on Water Street was a popular gathering place

Chinese and Canadian Dishes, Expertly Prepared,
Delivered to Your Door Piping Hot
FOR FREE HOME DELIVERY — 621-5110
GEORGES
Restaurant
21 Water St. N.
Galt

George's Restaurant continues to be a downtown mainstay

Woolworths lunch counter, a must-visit for Main Street shoppers

In Preston, there was The Skyway, a tiny diner that was a hold-out from the 1940's that remained popular throughout the 1960's.

The Skyway Restaurant, famous for their Lime Rickey soda pop

And who doesn't recall their many visits to the Dairy Queen on King Street and then sitting on the wall next door to enjoy your creamy treat and watch the cars drive by.

1¢ SALE
Get one for 1¢
with purchase
of one at
REGULAR PRICE!
THURSDAY
April 17th
ONE DAY
ONLY
ON ALL
SUNDAES
ONLY!
DAIRY QUEEN
328 King Street East
• STORE HOURS 12 NOON TO 11 P.M. •

The car enthusiasts in town were especially drawn towards several drive-in restaurants located in the community. Preston had the Knotty Pine, a coffee shop that transitioned over the years into a drive-in, and later into an inside seating-only restaurant.

HEY GANG

WE'RE NOW OPEN

WITH CAR-HOP SERVICE

Just flick your lights . . . and service will be given promptly • Then sit back and enjoy tempting food, prepared to your taste.

FOR AFTER THE "GAMES" OR "PARTYTIME"

It Is Always

CHICKEN DELIGHT

STOP IN OR CALL 653-6216 FOR

FREE DELIVERY

IN GALT AND PRESTON

• *Delivered In Oven Equipped Vans*

• Served in disposable heat-seal plates . . . just open and eat • Ideal for family gatherings, outdoor BBQ, unexpected guests, parties, or as a kitchen holiday for Mom • Ask about our special catering service

KNOTTY PINE DRIVE-IN

115 Fountain St. Preston Dial 653-6216

Along the King Street corridor was Tastee Freez and Rustler's Roost, with Carl's Drive-In located out on Eagle across the street from the Sunset Drive-In theatre.

Tastee Freez on King Street, next to "Presto" bowling lanes

Rustler's Roost, a long forgotten Preston drive-in

He slipped out to get a Terrific Meal at Carl's

Where You Get Fast and Courteous Service

CARL'S DRIVE-IN

Restaurant

Corner of Highway No. 24 and Eagle St. Preston

GO-KARTING

OPEN FROM 4:00 P.M. SAT. & SUN. FROM 1:00

Safe Fun For Kids
Fully Paved Track

Protective Helmets Supplied

KARTLAND

Next to Carl's Drive-In Corner of Eagle St. and Highway 24.

Carl's Drive-In & Kartland, across from Sunset Drive-In Theatre

Hespeler was served for many years by several wonderful "mom and pop" diners located throughout the downtown corridor. Kentucky Fried Chicken was the town's only fast food franchise, located smack dab in the middle of the Queen Street strip.

The Queen Street cruise along Hespeler's main drag was a must on a hot summer evening. From Ott's garage on one end to the turn around at the post office, cruising up and down Queen Street through downtown Hespeler was a fun excursion, especially at night.

Ott's Garage has been in operation since 1905

Galt had quite a variety of drive-in restaurants located throughout the city. Best remembered were "The Log Cabin Drive-In" and "The Thunderbird Frostop Drive-In", both located out on Hespeler Road, as well as "Brownie's Drive-In" at the top of the hill on St. Andrews Street, and "Henning's Drive-In", out on Clyde Road.

The Log Cabin Drive-In on Hespeler Road

Log Cabin was among the most popular drive-in restaurants in town. Featuring both indoor seating as well as car hop curb service, it was best known for a specialty foot-long hot dog they called "Underdog", with chopped tomatoes and onions added underneath the hot dog in the bun. Home cut French fries, cherry Cokes, and large hamburgers were also well remembered treats.

Log Cabin was located on Hespeler Road, which was at that time a narrow two-lane road that was not at all busy like it is today. There were very few other businesses along this strip back then, making the restaurant even more popular to teenagers and car enthusiasts due to its remote surroundings.

Local hot car enthusiasts would commonly gather together in the large parking lot outside "The Logs" on a warm summer night. You never knew what cars might show up.

Closed in the winter, Log Cabin's spring opening each year was celebrated throughout the city.

This wonderful "Mom and Pop" restaurant was owned and operated by Art and Ruby Young, who were known for their caring personalities. Whether you were an employee or a customer, they looked after the young patrons that often frequented their establishment.

While there was a thriving cruising scene at the Log Cabin, with plenty of hot car activity, the regulars knew better than to let things get out of hand. Art & Ruby were not afraid to confront any potential troublemakers head on, and few young people didn't take them seriously. Because of that understanding and respect, the Log Cabin remains a cherished memory for those that frequented this well-loved drive-in.

Thunderbird Frostop on Hespeler Road.
Royal Bank building in the background

The Frostop was located on Hespeler Road, north of the Log Cabin near Sheldon Street. The restaurant was actually called "The Thunderbird Drive-In Restaurant", which served Frostop Root Beer, but just about everyone referred to the place as Frostop.

Out on the edge of the street was a sign featuring a gigantic smiling snowman holding a frosty mug of root beer in his right hand and a hot dog in his left. The building was a large A-Frame design that had both inside seating and curb service with car hops, along with picnic tables surrounding the structure. There was plenty of parking in front, with an open field behind the building. Beside the restaurant was a popular miniature golf course, an attraction that was also operated by the Frostop owners Alf Snider and Don Carter.

Employees busily prepare food orders at Thunderbird Frostop

According to Donna McArthur, who worked for 4 years at the Hespeler Road Frostop as a car hop, being an employee was not like working at most other jobs. She thought of it more like hanging out with friends every evening, surrounded by a party-like atmosphere that certainly made her work shift a real pleasure during most nights.

Her work uniform included a brown trimmed pale yellow t-shirt with "Thunderbird Frostop" printed on the right, along with brown pants and white tennis shoes. To emphasize her point about this unique restaurant and what it meant to her to have worked there, even after 50 years, she proudly still owns her work shirt.

Donna McArthur's car hop shirt from the 1960's

The laid-back atmosphere at Frostop was popular with teens all over town, especially those from several local roller skating clubs. The restaurant became a well loved meeting place before and after long skating sessions at Preston, Hespeler, and Galt Arenas.

Inside the Hespeler Road Frostop Drive-In
12 members of Preston's "Rolling Rebels" roller skating club pose together after downing multiple mugs of Frostop root beer.

Thunderbird Frostop had a low-cost menu, including their very popular "T-Bird Special" consisting of a 2 piece chicken dinner, French fries, coleslaw and a mug of Frostop root beer for 99 cents.

Frostop car hop delivers food to customers in their cars

Many serious cruise enthusiasts would congregate on a regular basis at the “T-Bird”, making it a must visit for any car related extra curricular activity. With its remote location on Hespeler Road, many of these serious gearheads knew that there were several excellent side roads nearby for some short run street races. At that time, the remote back roads known as Townline Road and Pinebush Road were probably the most popular, and a short distance from the Frostop parking lot.

The Thunderbird Frostop was a magnet for hot cars in the 1960’s

Brownie's was another popular drive-in restaurant, located at the top of the hill on St. Andrews Street, as you headed towards the nearby town of Paris, Ontario. This west-side drive-in was popular for its close proximity to the downtown Galt cruising scene. Owned and operated by Bob Brown, the drive-in featured great burgers, fries, and creamy milkshakes.

Customers driving into the restaurant would read the outside menu board, then flash their headlights, signaling a Brownie's car hop that they were ready to order their food. Just inside the front doors were bar stools where customers could also eat at the counter. The restaurant had a small T.V. located inside above the counter, during the era when few people had televisions in their homes.

The night time view looking down the hill on St. Andrews Street after pulling out of Brownie's Drive-In. At the bottom of the hill is Cedar and Ainslie Streets, and the quickest way to Galt's downtown Cruise

As an added incentive to gather more customers, Bob Brown made the business decision to stay open during the winter months. As soon as the Log Cabin closed for the season in the fall, Brownie's management began an extensive advertising campaign in the Cambridge Reporter newspaper, hoping to lure disenfranchised Log Cabin customers to their St. Andrews Street drive-in restaurant.

Another popular place to cruise was one of the best. After venturing all around town, it was the choice of many to then head over to Clyde Road in Galt for a visit to Henning's Drive-In. The food was fabulous and the service was the best. Several prominent hot rod enthusiasts have expressed to me that Henning's was their preferred choice. "My buddies and I would hang out at Frostop and The Log Cabin to show off our cars, but we always ended the evening with a visit to Henning's for a Banquet Burger and fries with gravy".

Henning's Drive-In at 230 Clyde Road in Galt

Theresa and Oscar Henning

This popular restaurant was operated by Oscar and Theresa Henning, a hard-working couple that brought a new standard of quality and service to the local drive-in restaurant business.

While their daughter Carla Henning and her friend Lee Waring were car hops, providing a special brand of customer service, the job of preparing the food on the Henning's menu fell strictly on the shoulders of Theresa and Oscar.

Car hop Carla Henning during a rare day off

Henning's car hop Lee Waring having fun with friends Paul Mason and Jim Drew outside the restaurant in 1966

During down time, Carla and Lee were often busy preparing fresh potatoes to be cut into French fries, an equally important job that upheld the restaurant's sterling reputation of freshly prepared quality food. During the 1960's, Henning's was the epitome of the "Mom and Pop" fresh food drive-in restaurant, with a unique charm that won over the many customers that frequented the establishment.

Key to the success of Henning's legendary fries was due to this Leland-brand French fry potato cutter, a wall mounted device that cut fresh potatoes into enormous fries. The actual cutter used at Henning's in the 1960's is now in the possession of a private collector in Galt.

Theresa Henning cooking burgers on the grill

While popular with families and young people, the many car enthusiasts in town found that a trip to Henning's quickly and easily became a daily ritual. It wasn't lost on these enthusiasts that not only was the food top quality in taste, the Henning's car hops took special notice of each of the cars that appeared in the parking lot. According to car hop Lee Waring, both she and Carla got to know the owners of many of the various custom cars that constantly filled the parking lot, with the ability to recognize the name and model of each car brand. Another feature that made such a difference is that these car hops also understood how particular hot rod enthusiasts can be. If a customer pulled into the lot driving a regular vehicle, a tray full of food was hooked onto the window in typical era fashion. Realizing how special the custom cars were that showed up on a regular basis, the Henning's car hops would instinctively hand the food to the car owners instead of trusting the window tray, reassuring the "car guys" there was never a disastrous drink spill inside the car. This thoughtful move endeared the car hops to the many car enthusiasts, creating a bond beyond anything experienced at any other local drive-in restaurant.

Garth Wood relaxes at a table inside Henning's Drive-In

Galt resident Peter Scott and his award winning 1963 Corvette

Early Corvette from Doerner Speed & Custom Shop on Jaffray Street

Larry Clayton's Hemi Cuda

Pat Gillies Pontiac Firebird

The location of the previously mentioned drive-in restaurants created the logical route for many of the serious cruising enthusiasts. The most adventurous cruisers drove through the entire circuit in town. Starting with a visit to Log Cabin on Hespeler Road, the northbound drive down that stretch of road led you to Frostop, near the corner of Hespeler Road and Sheldon Street. Leaving the parking lot after your visit, you would drive further north and turn left onto Eagle Street. On your left was Carl's Drive-In. On the right was the Sunset Drive-In.

Sunset Drive-In on Eagle Street

Continuing along Eagle Street, it was a bit of a drive until you finally reached King Street in Preston. Turning left onto King, the Dairy Queen was located on the right. The King Street section of the cruise was a lot of fun, with stores and shops on both sides of the street all lit up with neon signs.

King Street in downtown Preston

Presto Bowling Lanes on King Street, the home of 5 pin bowling

Traveling south on King as the road becomes Coronation Boulevard, you travel past Loblaws on the left, and the golf course and hospital on the right. Coronation is actually a portion of old Highway 8, which crosses Highway 24. This major intersection is known locally as the Delta.

Turning right on Highway 24, you would be traveling along Water Street heading into Galt's downtown section. On Water Street, you would have passed by the Grand Theatre at Dickson Street, and the Capitol Theatre, a bit further south past Main Street.

The Grand Theatre on Water Street across from the Post Office

The Capitol Theatre in Water Street, south of Main

A cruise through downtown Galt was a tradition that carried on for decades. While not necessarily that long of a circuit, it was very popular with many cruising enthusiasts during the 1960's.

High Park Texaco, a centrally located service station at the corner of Main and Shade Streets became the natural starting point and subsequent turnaround area for the downtown cruise.

Two points need to be made regarding this Texaco Station. Not only was it the perfect opportunity to fill the tank before spending time driving up and down Main Street, but the gas station's pop cooler full of ice cold soft drinks was always a big hit during a hot and humid summer evening.

Downtown Galt's cruise route started at High Park Texaco

Action along Main Street in downtown Galt

From the Texaco Station at Main and Shade Streets, driving down Main took you past all of the major downtown stores and restaurants, as well as The Palace, a fabulous Art Deco movie theatre located right on Main Street.

The Palace Theatre on Main Street

Major downtown department stores included both Walkers and The Right House. Raymond's Nut Shop was everyone's first choice for treats. The company later evolved into today's Reid's Chocolates.

Raymond's Nut Shop on Main Street

Clothing stores included Barton's Men's Wear, where every hot rodder in Ontario got special pricing deals on car club jackets and crests. The store was the official supplier to the A.T.A.O., Ontario's early drag racing association.

BARTON'S MEN'S WEAR

51 MAIN ST. GALT, ONT.

PHONE 244

Specializing in Club Jackets

A WIDE VARIETY OF STYLES AND CRESTS ARE AVAILABLE FEATURING A SPECIAL DISCOUNT FOR CLUBS.

THE OFFICIAL SUPPLIER FOR A.T.A.O.
T-SHIRTS ETC.

Supplier for the Automobile Timing Association of Ontario

Main Street looking down towards Queen's Square

As you crossed Water Street and drove over the Main Street bridge, cruisers circled around Queen's Square to head back downtown.

Main Street's arched bridge

The YMCA building, the home of popular "Teen Town" dances, was located across from Queen's Square. This became a very popular part of the Main Street cruise, especially as the dances were over and the crowds were leaving.

Circle around Queen's Square and head back downtown
The YMCA building is to the left

About the same time of night, the movie crowds were leaving the Capitol and the Grand Theatres on Water Street, and the Palace patrons were also leaving that theatre on Main Street. With throngs of young people spilling out onto the streets all about the same time, what better way to show off your car to the biggest audiences in town each evening.

Cruising along Water Street, about to cross Main Street

Carload of young people having fun cruising on Water Street

For the most part, these popular cruising destinations of the 1950's and '60's are gone today. In Preston, Carl's Drive-In, Rustler's Roost and Tastee Freez have all closed. The Skyway is now the Cambridge Restaurant. The lone survivor from those days is the Dairy Queen on King Street.

In Hespeler, the Kentucky Fried Chicken has closed its original downtown location and moved to a new outlet on Holiday Inn Drive. Ott's Garage, which first opened in 1905 is actually still in operation in Hespeler.

In Galt, the Frostop closed down and was converted to an A&W Drive-In, surviving until the early 1990's before finally closing.

The Log Cabin closed after the city expropriated the property to extend Dunbar Road that cut right through the area which held the popular restaurant. Art and Ruby Young's original plans were to open an all new Log Cabin location on Pinebush Road, but those plans ultimately fell through. The undeveloped restaurant property on Pinebush was then sold to the members of the Motor Lords Car Club, where they built their extensive clubhouse building on the site, a structure which still stands today.

Bob Brown closed Brownie's Drive-In and moved to nearby Paris, Ontario, where he opened a variety store.

Henning's on Clyde Road remained popular for several decades. After the family closed their drive-in and sold the property, it became Little Louie's for a brief time. The original building still stands today but is currently empty.

Cruising activity in the complex city of Cambridge is still enjoyed by a few dedicated enthusiasts but is not nearly as prevalent as it was during its heyday in the 1960's.

Shared memories from the following: Tim Cross, Pat Gillies, Larry Ray, Murray Harnack, Michael Dalton, Al Howlett, Warren Grimm, Donna McArthur, Wendy Lewin, Barbara Heagy, Carol Dahmer, Marilyn Geldart Van Horn, Gloria Wismer Cloutier, Donna Wittier, Jim Dawson, Anne Brown, Sam Vincent, Moya Clair-Howell, Fred Leber, Elaine Sharkey, Elizabeth Gray, Jill C. Armstrong Searson, Donna LaCroix, Peter Pisarchuk, Archie Ginson, June Legue, Howard Steel, Howie Hill, Donald and Rosemary Eaton, Peggy Sue Rivers, Orval Stortz, Bob Reain, Marilyn Riddell Gibbons, George Lawrence Wingham, Judee Richardson Schofield, Rita Ringo, Tom Hogg, Colleen Hutchinson, and the gang at the "Memories of Galt-Preston-Hespeler" Facebook group.

Special thank you to the following: Carla Henning, Joy Henning Moon, Dan Schmalz, Cambridge Archives, Lee Waring Kools, Sandy and Hal Tilley, Bob Jones, Peter Coutts, Sally Stewart, Ross Reid, Cambridge Public Library, Carrie Drew-Smith, and Alek Livingstone.

CHAPTER THREE
Delhi, Simcoe, Courtland & Tillsonburg

Tobacco farms surround the entire Norfolk County

Delhi is a small farming community in the heart of tobacco country. Surrounded by thousands of acres of tobacco farms, the sleepy community seems as unlikely a cruising hot spot as could be imagined. As anyone who grew up in this area can tell you though, you can't assume anything. Overlook the obvious, because there are more than a few surprises to be discovered here.

Downtown Delhi

Even though there wasn't a whole lot of places to cruise to in town, there was still a vibrant cruising environment. Delhi is centrally located exactly 12 miles between the larger communities of Simcoe to the east, and Tillsonburg to the west. In between, there was a marvelous opportunity to shake up your need for speed, as well as the chance to cruise more than one route on any given evening.

Locals meet up with seasonal farm workers in downtown Delhi

With more than a few eager diehard cruisers in town, the nighttime became the right time to hit the strip. Directly through the centre of town was Highway 3, known locally as "The Four Lanes".

It was common place for the occasional heavy right foot to fall directly on a gas pedal somewhere on Main Street. “Stop light” drag races were typical, from the east end of town to the natural turn around at Wills Motors for a return spin through town, with a constant watch of activity at the local police station. After all, there is no need to stir up the local constabulary who may suddenly become unnecessarily interested in any hot car activity in town.

If specific cruise destinations were few and far between in small town Delhi, what the community did have was the Belgian Club, a night club in town that featured some of the biggest recording acts of the day playing live in person. The large concert hall was sold out each night a big act was booked, becoming a regular stop on the tour circuit for many musical acts during the 1960's.

The Belgian Club in downtown Delhi

Roy Orbison on stage at Delhi's Belgian Club

DELHI BELGIAN CLUB presents . . .

PARADE OF STARS

SATURDAYS

Dancing 8:30 - 12:00

SATURDAY, NOVEMBER 5
LITTLE CAESAR AND THE CONSULS
SINGING THEIR LATEST: "Mercy, Mr. Percy"
Also Starring: The MOOD GROUP

SATURDAY, NOVEMBER 12
THE WINDJAMMERS
PLUS: The Sir David Quintet

SATURDAY, NOVEMBER 19
ROBBIE LANE
and the
DISCIPLES
FROM:
THE TV SHOW
'It's Happening'
With The A-Go-Go Girls

Saturday, Nov. 26
THE
Barbarians
PLUS:
Sir David Quintet
ADMISSION $2.00 A Person

SATURDAY, DECEMBER 3
THE FIVE GOOD REASONS
and The MOOD GROUP

SATURDAY, DECEMBER 10
THE 'EXPLOSIVE SOUND' OF
BOBBY KRIS AND THE IMPERIALS

SATURDAY, DECEMBER 17
10 PIECE POWERFUL ORCHESTRA
THE MAJESTICS

SATURDAY, DECEMBER 24
CHRISTMAS EVE DANCE
DANCING 8:30 - 11:30
THE DELEGATES WITH GO-GO GIRLS

SATURDAY, DECEMBER 31
NEW YEAR'S EVE DANCE
8 PIECE GROUP THE PLAGUES
ADMISSION $2.50 Per Person

IN THE

Shield and Friend Room

MEMBERS AND GUESTS ONLY

NOVEMBER 5
The Hilarious 4½ TONNERS
Lawrence Ferris and his Orchestra

NOVEMBER 12
Marcel and Lawrence Trio
Featuring: M. Dnee — Virtuoso Accordionist

NOVEMBER 19
Marcel and Lawrence Trio
Featuring: Kathy Lee Jackson

NOVEMBER 26
Marcel and Lawrence Trio
Guest Appearance by The BARBARIANS

DECEMBER 3
Lawrence Ferris and his Orchestra

DECEMBER 10
RAYMOND and his 6 piece Belgian Orchestra

DECEMBER 17
From London
The Sensational BOOMERANGS

DECEMBER 24

DECEMBER 31

KATHY LEE JACKSON

SUNDAYS

Dancing 8:30 - 12:00

NOVEMBER 6
LITTLE CAESAR
and The CONSULS
PLUS:
SIR DAVID QUINTET

SUNDAY, NOVEMBER 13
The Sensational Toronto Special
L. E. SPENCER AND THE POWER
ALSO:
THE MOOD GROUP

SUNDAY, NOVEMBER 20
'The Explosive Sound' of
BOBBY Kris
and The IMPERIALS
ALSO FEATURING:
THE SIR DAVID QUINTET

SUNDAY, NOVEMBER 27
The 'Orbeson Sound' OF
BOB BOUCHARD
and THE ENCHANTERS
PLUS: The Mood Group

SUNDAY, DECEMBER 4
THE FIVE GOOD REASONS
ALSO: The Sir David Quintet

SUNDAY, DECEMBER 11
Once Again 'The Explosive Sound' Of
BOBBY KRIS AND THE IMPERIALS

SUNDAY, DECEMBER 18
Detroit's Top Night Club Orchestra
THE DEL-RAYS

NO DANCE CHRISTMAS DAY

SUNDAY, JANUARY 1
New Year's Day
The Sensational COACHMEN

SEMI - FORMAL DRESS REQUIRED AT ALL DANCES

Delhi Belgian Club Ltd.
YOUR CENTRE OF ENTERTAINMENT

Parade of Stars live in concert in downtown Delhi, Ontario

In the early 1960's, nearby Tillsonburg had a population of about six thousand residents, while Simcoe was slightly less than this. Delhi cruisers certainly got the best of all worlds by having both of those communities within a few miles of town. If nothing seemed to be going on in one of those towns, it was a quick trip over to the other to check out the action.

Exploring each community finds a wealth of quality cruising destinations and several great hangouts for the local gearheads of Norfolk County.

Courtland, Ontario

On a date with your special someone? You were probably on your way to the Skylark Drive-In Theatre in nearby Courtland, Ontario. After the show, you could drive across the street to the Diamond Drive-In Restaurant for their selection of great food and treats. Another charming restaurant available to anyone in the Courtland area was the Pleasant Acre Drive-In, just west of town.

Skylark Drive-In Theatre in nearby Courtland

DIAMOND DRIVE - IN

CORNER No. 3 AND No. 59 HIGHWAYS

Invite You To Visit Them

Featuring . . .

Flavor Crisp Kentucky Chicken

* SOFT ICE CREAM   * HOME-MADE HARD ICE CREAM

* CATERING TO OUTSIDE PARTIES

TAKE OUT SERVICE   **PHONE 842-2628**

Dining at the Diamond Drive-In in Courtland

THE PLEASANT ACRE DRIVE IN

Fish and Chips

59¢

Hamburgs

29¢

HOT DINNERS **99¢**
Beverage Included

Children's Portions
Half Price

Specials Fri. and Sat. Only

TABLE SERVICE
OR
EAT IN YOUR CAR

TAKE OUT
OR
PHONE IN
ORDERS

UNDER NEW MANAGEMENT
842-4472
No. 3 Highway 2 Miles West Courtland

Pleasant Acre Drive-In Restaurant near Courtland

GLEN-MUR DRIVE-IN

WHERE THE YOUNG AT HEART LOVE TO EAT

519 N. Broadway

As you drove further down the road, one of several must-visits would be the Glen-Mur Drive-In, located at 519 Broadway Street in Tillsonburg. Known locally as one of the city's premier cruising destinations, the Glen-Mur featured great food, a genuine home-town atmosphere, and a rockin' jukebox full of the latest hit songs.

Inside the Glen-Mur Drive-In

Other popular Tillsonburg drive-in restaurants include Scotty's Drive-In, as well as the A&J Drive-In, known for their home-made ice cream and their own special root beer.

Scotty's Drive-In, an early Tillsonburg hot spot

A and J DRIVE-IN

Featuring

Homemade Hard and Soft Ice Cream

Snack and Meals A & J Root Beer

AL AND JUDIE ATKINSON

(Prop.)

No. 19 Highway South Tillsonburg

You have been assisted by a member of the

Tillsonburg Flywheels

A Hot Rod Club formed by a group of young men dedicated to automobile safety and presenting to the public the meaning of their sport.

Sponsored by

STALEY'S GARAGE

Tillsonburg, Ontario

7 Young Street **Phone VI 2-3192**

The Flywheels were an early hot rod car club based in Tillsonburg. Many of the members could be seen cruising in town throughout the summer season

Various Flywheel club members and their cars

Hot rods and custom cars of the Flywheels Car Club in Tillsonburg

Pearce Motors was a favourite place to gather any time of year

Hard working craftsmen could be found at LaPlante Body Shop

There was always lots going on at Tillsonburg Tire & Battery

Tillsonburg's High School parking lot was typically full of hot cars

After school, many could be found here

The Tillsonburg hot car fraternity finally had a true destination location when an A&W Drive-In opened at 116 Simcoe Street. This popular burger haven instantly became the central meet-up place in town, featuring the hottest cars in the area. There were few evenings in the summer that this parking lot was not a constant beehive of activity.

The most popular cruise route in Tillsonburg during the 1960's was the drive between the Glen-Mur Drive-In on Broadway, and the A&W Drive-In on Simcoe Street.

This popular cruise through town led you from the A&W parking lot on Simcoe Street, turning west towards the downtown business district. Turn right onto Broadway and enjoy the slow cruise along the strip with its store fronts all lit up with neon signs.

Continuing along Broadway, the drive takes you out of the downtown core and into a residential area as you make your way towards the Glen-Mur Drive-in. As you turn left into the Glen-Mur parking lot, you had to stop and enjoy the food and hospitality offered at this local landmark.

Always lots of action in downtown Tillsonburg

Downtown Tillsonburg at night

On the evenings that you needed a change of atmosphere, you could join the other nearby cruise through the city of Simcoe.

Downtown Simcoe

The short 12 mile journey from Delhi meant that you would be driving along Highway 3 that becomes The Queensway in Simcoe.

Angle parking in downtown Simcoe

Looking both ways on Norfolk through downtown Simcoe

SIMCOE ARENA

ROLLER SKATING

During

"OLD HOME WEEK-END"

FRIDAY, AUGUST 4th — 8 - 10.30 p.m.

SATURDAY, AUGUST 5th

ROLLER SKATING and DANCE

Skating 7.30 to 9.30 — Dance 9 to 11.45

Admission $1.00

SUNDAY, AUGUST 6th — 8 to 10 p.m.

ROLLER SKATING

Lots of activities to keep Simcoe teenagers busy

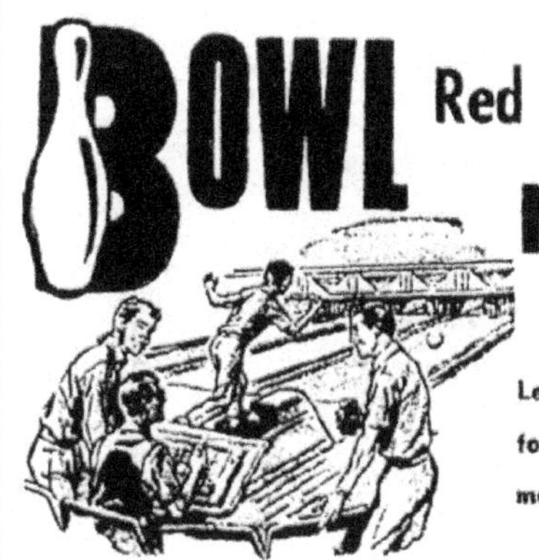

Red Kelly Bowling Lanes

NOW OPEN

For The 1967-68 Season On

League secretaries and bowlers wishing to form new leagues are asked to contact the management as early as possible.

Open Evenings — Monday Through Saturday During September

Open Sundays

Openings Available For Leagues

DIAL 426-2414 or 587-4103

Persons interested in joining a League, contact the Alley.

BOWL

ATTENTION

BOWLERS!

"Bowl at Your Best in Our Alleys"

Now is the time, openings available to arrange for times and to form your teams, in Ladies' or Men's leagues.

LEAGUES TO START BY SEPT. 15th

We have refinished our alleys, purchased new pins and installed "electric eye" foul lines to add to your bowling pleasure.

Alleys Now Available for Open Bowling

— Come and try them Now! —

STAR RECREATION

Robinson St. Simcoe GA 6-0001

AL FREEMAN'S

Dominion Tire Store

- Complete Mechanical Service
- Wheel Alignment
- Sporting Goods

"Service Is Character In Action"

Located at

NORFOLK STREET NORTH

At Airline Tracks

Simcoe

Gulf service station, Colborne and Peel Streets in Simcoe

Simcoe's main cruising destination was the A&W Drive-In, on the corner of Queensway (Highway 3) and Norfolk Street (Highway 24). Talk about the centre of activity, this was the hub of cruising in Simcoe. This major intersection would also point you in the direction of the nearby beach communities of Long Point, Turkey Point, and Port Dover, just a few miles from town.

Car hops were busy at Simcoe's A&W Drive-In

The typical Simcoe cruise route would start at the A&W on Queensway at Norfolk. After circling through the parking lot, the journey leads you down Norfolk towards the downtown core, where you would cruise up and down along the main storefront shopping streets of Robinson and Colborne before joining back up with Norfolk. The other necessary cruising destination included a stop at the Tastee Treat Drive-In, located at 426 Norfolk Street South.

Did you know the Tastee Treat serves many Mouth-Watering Goodies as well as Ice Cream, Sundaes and Shakes?

TREAT YOUR FAMILY TO ONE OF THE FOLLOWING:

- DEEP FRIED FANTAIL SHRIMP
- HONEY FRIED CHICKEN "FIT FOR A COLONEL"
- JUICY CORNED BEEF ON A BUN
- OUR ORIGINAL BACON BURG SPECIALTY (4 Slices of Bacon on a Fancy Bun with Tomato and Lettuce)
- OUR SPECIAL SUBMARINE SANDWICHES
- DELICIOUS FOOTLONGS, CHEESEBURGS, HAMBURGS, DIXIE DOGS AND CHICKEN-ON-A-BUN

FRIDAY SPECIAL **FISH & CHIPS** Deep Fried Ocean Haddock with Golden French Fries **55c**

Bring Along This Ad This Wednesday For A Free Sundae Of Your Choice

TASTEE TREAT

426 NORFOLK STREET SOUTH SIMCOE 426-4896

Free Delivery on Orders Over $3.00 Open Year Round

Large menu at the Tastee Treat in Simcoe

For people still willing to enjoy these old cruise routes through Delhi, Simcoe, Courtland and Tillsonburg, they can still be followed for the most part through each of these communities. If you are willing to open your mind and stretch your imagination a bit, today's car enthusiasts can still seek out a very enjoyable journey, following in the footsteps of yesterday's cruising enthusiasts through Ontario's tobacco belt.

A special thank you goes out to my friend and fellow old car enthusiast **Randy Goudeseune** for his memories of many hot car adventures in his home town of Delhi.

Also, **thank you** to the many members of the "Remembering Tillsonburg", the "I Grew Up in Courtland", and the "If You Grew Up in Simcoe" Facebook groups for all of their help.

CHAPTER FOUR
Guelph

Nighttime view of downtown Guelph

Guelph is one of those small Ontario cities that seemed to have everything a modern family of the 1950's could need. The city offered historic buildings, a robust downtown, fun nightlife, beautiful parks and a warm inviting vibe throughout the entire town. For young people, the cruising scene was vibrant, with lots of great downtown activity during both day and night, and a wide variety of places to go to in town to hang out with your buddies.

One of the earliest gathering spots was Rocky's Drive-In at 520 Elizabeth Street. Established in 1951 and renowned for their gourmet hot dogs, a Guelph summer was never complete without a visit to Rocky's.

Rocky's Drive-In on Elizabeth Street, a Guelph landmark since 1951

A&W opened their first Guelph Drive-In location at 587 York Road, a short two minute drive from Rocky's. With the close proximity of both of these food establishments, the trip back and forth between both drive-ins became the first serious cruising circuit in town.

Guelph's first A&W Drive-In on York Road

Staff picture at the York Road A&W Drive-In

The variety of food items was greater at A&W with the added luxury and convenience of car hop curb service and a larger parking lot. Rocky's had the longer history which kept the crowds returning time and time again. Having both drive-ins so close to each other, there was a natural rivalry between the two establishments.

Another series of popular meeting places in Guelph included the Dairy Queen, a storied fast food franchise, as well as the Golden T Drive-In, which operated the first local Kentucky Fried Chicken franchise in Guelph.

Downtown, there were several popular places, including the Green Rooster on Carden Street, the lunch counter at Woolworths, and the fabulous Treanon Restaurant, at the corner of Wyndam and Macdonell Streets. Inside this wonderful downtown restaurant, the booths were cozy and intimate, the coffee was fresh, and the great burgers, hand cut fries and delicious homemade pies were mouth watering and memorable.

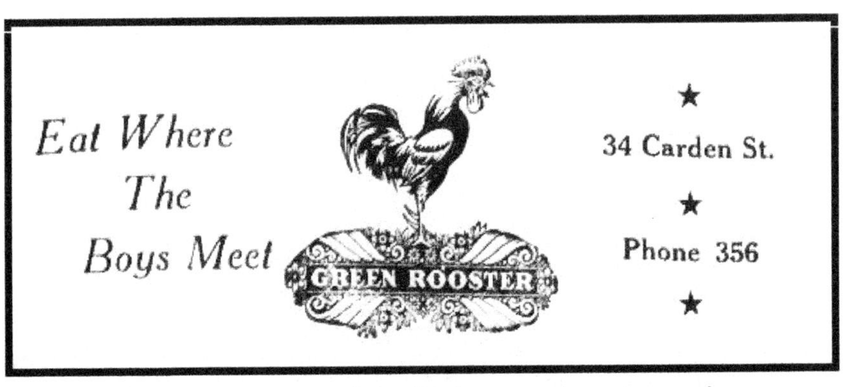

Green Rooster was popular with hungry downtown shoppers

Lunch counter inside Woolworths (left) was another favourite

Treanon Restaurant, at the corner of Wyndam and Macdonell

Booth and counter service inside the Treanon Restaurant

By 1959, Harvey's opened up one of their earliest franchise locations at 12 Gordon Street, which became a new favourite destination close to the downtown cruising action.

One important gathering spot for serious car enthusiasts was Ed Schell's Sunoco station on the corner of Fife and Highway 24. Schell was not only a well respected mechanic, but encouraged others to bring their specialty vintage vehicles to the shop. On any given day, there were all kinds of hot rods, restored classics, and muscle cars parked outside.

Schell's Sunoco, one of Guelph's finest "car guy" hangouts

Don Havers also opened up his speed shop on Highway 7, not far away from Schell's station, becoming another favourite gathering place for motor enthusiasts. Havers was known for his very fast Ford Falcon, setting elapsed times and speed records at several drag strips in Ontario in 1965.

Don Haver's Ford Falcon in action at St. Thomas Dragway

LLOYD'S SPEED SHOP

- SPORTS and SMALL CAR ACCESSORIES
- RODS
- CUSTOMS
- MOTORCYCLE SALES and SERVICE
- GOKARTS
- SPEED EQUIPMENT
- CUSTOM PAINTING

LLOYD'S SPEED SHOP
CLEARVIEW AVE.
R.R. No. 2, GUELPH, ONTARIO
Phone TAylor 2-1540

Lloyd's Speed Shop on Clearview Avenue

ROAMERS

GUELPH

Roamers, an early rod and custom car club

Roamers club house located behind Harvey's

In the early 1950's, one diversion from the downtown cruise circuit was a trip to the Jem Drive-In, located on Speedvale Avenue near Stevenson.

Downtown Guelph

That downtown cruise circuit included trips up and down Wyndam Street, making sure you drove past the lineups of movie patrons at the front doors of the Odeon Theatre. Necessary journeys along streets like Carden, Macdonell, Baker and Quebec streets, interwove a deliberate pattern to pass in front of every busy store front and business throughout the downtown core.

Mildly customized 1950 Mercury cruising Carden Street

Lowered white 1959 Ford parked on Wyndam Street

Since not everyone had a car to drive, creative teenagers chose the next logical solution by simply congregating at what was known as the "See Spot", a collection of bus benches surrounding the downtown square. From this location, the endless parade of young people in automobiles out enjoying the summer evening could be taken in with the widest field of view.

Cruising through downtown Guelph at night

By the early 1970's, A&W had already opened a second, more modern drive-in restaurant location on Woodlawn Road. With the increased population growth in Guelph, it was no surprise to also witness the opening of The Red Barn and Burger Chef, which competed with other long established eateries like the Alpine Drive-In during this same time frame. These locations all became part of a later era cruising circuit in Guelph.

A&W Drive-In on Woodlawn Road in Guelph

Updated Dairy Queen on Woolwich

Red Barn Restaurant on Norfolk Street

15 cent hamburgers at the Burger Chef

Now, 50 years later, the cruising era has long ended in Guelph. The Jem Drive-In property on Speedsvale Road was redeveloped into a strip mall surrounded by suburban housing. Fortunately, Guelph's Mustang Drive-In Theatre remains as one of the few theatres of its kind still operating in the province. The A&W Drive-Ins on York Road and on Woodlawn have both closed, as well as the Red Barn on Norfolk, and the Golden T on Woolwich. It was an especially sad day in Guelph when the Treanon Restaurant closed its doors.

Surprisingly enough, even after 70 years in business, Rocky's Drive-In, the venerable hot dog emporium on Elizabeth Street is still in operation. The original Harvey's on Gordon Street is also still in operation after more than 60 years.

The new retro-styled A&W on Wellington harkens back to those early days of car hop curb service out on York Road, but now with the modern conveniences of today's drive-thru window. Yes, it's a compromise, but you can never truly go back to what once was.

Shared memories by the following: Kim Elliot Coles, James Leslie, Sharon Kreller, Carol Anne Kentner, Mary Lynch-Ficioris, Ken Waechter, Ray Reilly, John Swartzenburg, Mary Anne Mitchell, Marion Keleher, Kevin Lowry, Marlene Thompson, Brenda Burgoon, Kathy Lawrence, Jo Parisoto Lomas, Suzy Hebden, Robert Penfold, Lois Moersch Dykstra, Charlie Burton, Janice Marples-Goodwin, Tom Douglas, Steve Twine, Joe Davies, Marg Robb, Robert Clayton, Bruce Gilbert, Lynda Vollett, Anne Kinch, Earl Evans, Ross Morrow, Brian Ramsay, Marilyn Metcalf, Colleen Lawler DeBoer, Sebastian Dal Bo, Susan Demeter, Terry Bolger, Sandy Semple, Neil Dudley, Barry Bevan, Edith Gopsill, Marti Sharpe, Lynn Couling, Mike Baker, John Bower, Sandi Smythe-Tovell, Joan Byron, Patricia Whitechurch, Glen Moores, Carol Cowtan, and John Leithead.

Special thanks to: Guelph Museum, and the generous members of the "If you grew up in Guelph" Facebook group.

CHAPTER FIVE
Hamilton

CKOC was one of two rock and roll radio stations in Hamilton

During the middle of the 20th century, Hamilton, Ontario was well known for its steel factories located along the shoreline of Lake Ontario. Good paying jobs in the steel industry, plus the related spin-off jobs became the key drawing card for the population of hard working men and women of Hamilton. Several generations of Hamiltonians relied on the steel factories to provide them with a steady income. With a successful cash flow, there was more than enough interest in car activity to keep the youthful Hamiltonian gear heads busy within several distinct areas of the city. As early as the beginning part of the 1950's that would last through to well into the 1970's, there were pockets of favourite cruising locations throughout greater Hamilton, making for a unique and memorable legacy in the history of automotive folklore.

Slow cruise along Beach Boulevard

On any given summer weekend in the 1950's, the place to cruise and be seen was along the lakeshore of Burlington Beach. What better place to be than this laidback community along the sandy shoreline of Lake Ontario. On one side of Beach Boulevard was a full fledged amusement park, and across the street was the beach. For car enthusiasts, the narrow two lane stretch of pavement and the close proximity of buildings and sidewalk made for a perfect slow cruise destination, giving spectators a good look at the cars driving by, and a great place to show off your car. In the middle of the action was The Angus Inn, a popular drive-in restaurant known for its quality food at reasonable prices. This was summer cruising at its best.

Endless cruising on a summer day

Angus Inn was a very popular stop along the beach cruise

At the same time, several miles up the road became the focus of other enthusiasts with some of the faster cars in town. Located on the corner of Highway 6 and Highway 5, known locally as Clappison's Corner was a charming and distinctive diner called The B-Hive.

The distinctive and unique B-Hive Restaurant at Clappison's Corners

The draw of this eatery was not just the especially tasty food and ample parking. Surrounded by acres of farm fields, the diner's remote location, and direct access to Highway 5's straight stretch of fresh pavement was an open invitation for illegal street racing. For several years, this became a preferred nighttime proving ground for early Hamiltonian performance enthusiasts.

B-Hive next to Highway 5, Hamilton's proving grounds

During the height of this era, a new car club emerged in town with a different approach. The Kustoms of Hamilton club was formed in the belief that cruising the streets in a custom car was an art form worthy of study and development. The whole philosophy of this group was to be seen sitting in the front seat of your lowered car, crawling along the street at a snails' pace. The average pedestrian would witness a spotless and dazzling street custom, with gleaming paint and chrome, spotless interiors, and the added low rumble of a V8 voiced through "Hollywood" mufflers. As hip as that image is, now increase the whole cool factor by including a dozen club cars, cruising the same street all at the same time.

1957 Meteor ragtop belonged to club president Ken Fraser.

Jerry Keith's super smooth street custom

Typical mild custom that was seen prowling Hamilton streets

Carl Gillespie's 1934 Plymouth coupe

As the city grew in population, automobile traffic began to overwhelm older and narrower sections of the downtown district. In 1956, to alleviate traffic flow issues, many streets in the core were designated one way streets, creating a more natural traffic flow, and providing the unintentional perfect scenario for cruising the downtown area.

For the custom car and hot rod enthusiast, Hamilton had more than its share of places to cruise to during this era. During the 1950's and into the 1960's, each major road within the city limits included an above average number of drive-in restaurants and diners all catering towards the youthful car enthusiast. Over on Barton Street, was the emergence of Harvey's and Dairy Queen, while KFC opened on both Upper James and on King Street.

3 LOCATIONS IN HAMILTON

HARVEY'S FOODS LIMITED • A PUBLIC COMPANY
OWNED AND OPERATED BY CANADIANS

Harvey's Drive-In, a Hamilton staple since 1959

The original Dairy Queen on Barton Street

A&W also opened four drive-in restaurant locations throughout greater Hamilton, becoming the main focus of extra curricular car activities on the streets of the steel city.

Out on Queenston Road, the new A&W location naturally brought in business from the local car enthusiasts. To help boost new business, an added attraction was having a popular local disc jockey on Hamilton's rock radio station 900 CHML, broadcast his show live from the restaurant. With Mike Marshall broadcasting his show each night along with the parking lot full of the hottest cars in the city, the A&W instantly became the place to be. Due to the overwhelming acceptance and popularity, other A&W locations were opened up on King Street in the downtown core, on Plains Road East in nearby Burlington, and another out on Upper James near Mohawk.

Queenston Road A&W with card in window about live radio shows

900 CHML DJ Mike Marshall

AT ALL FOUR LOCATIONS
IN THE HAMILTON AREA

744 QUEENSTON RD.
(STONEY CREEK)
PHONE 547-0785

959 UPPER JAMES
(ABOVE MOHAWK)
PHONE 389-0832

145 PLAINS RD. EAST
BURLINGTON
PHONE 634-5712

190 KING ST. WEST
(NEAR CAROLINE)
PHONE 529-1440

CALL AHEAD

FOR FAST PICKUP

the difference is delicious

Soon after A&W opened their drive-in on Queenston Road, Hamiltonians saw the emergence of the first Millionaire Drive-Inn, a stylish restaurant with canopy and car hop service, a wider variety of food options than A&W, and a giant neon sign impossible not to see.

THE Millionaire DRIVE INN LTD.

Under the canopy at the Millionaire Drive-Inn

Car hops on duty at the Millionaire Drive-Inn

As soon as the A&W on Upper James was opened, the owners of the Millionaire built another of their own, again just a short distance away. With both car hop drive-in restaurants operating at the same time, not only was the competition between restaurants intense, it was a bonanza of hot car activity for more than a decade and a half. The amount of cruising activity within the city of Hamilton was at an all-time high during this period.

The Millionaire Drive-Inn in action on Upper James & Mohawk

With two great places to hang out, it was natural to drive through the parking lot of the A&W, then venture down the street to the Millionaire and back again. It seems more than a coincidence that it was exactly a quarter mile between the A&W Drive-In and the Millionaire Drive-Inn on Queenston Road. Which drive-in had the hottest cars? That is like asking which drive-in had the best food. It depends on who you talk to. Either way, it was a constant rolling car show on any given summer evening at both restaurants.

Hot car central at this Hamilton area A&W Drive-In

More adventuress cruisers made the entire circuit, starting at the A&W at 959 Upper James, down the street to the Millionaire on the corner of Upper James at Mohawk. After cruising through both parking lots, head towards the downtown to the Harvey's on King at McNab and the nearby A&W at 188 King. Then venture back to Main Street, heading east towards Queenston to tour through both A&W and the Millionaire Drive-Ins. This one-way pass of the circuit was approximately 10 miles in length from start to finish, and would take about 40 minutes to complete.

Cruising action on King Street between A&W and Harvey's

Sadly, these great old cruising destinations of Hamilton's past are mostly gone today. Both locations of the great Millionaire Drive-Inn have been demolished, replaced today with strip plazas. The Harvey's location on King and McNab is now part of an office complex. The B'Hive was torn down decades ago and finally replaced with a Tim Horton's location. That stretch of Highway 5 once so popular with street racers is a much busier highway today and no longer out in the boondocks, with plenty of business development in the area. Along the Burlington Beach strip, the Angus Inn and the entire amusement park is gone, with the Burlington Skyway now overshadowing the beach front area. After closing the A&W Drive-Ins on King, Queenston Road and Upper James, back in the 1980's, there has been a revival of sorts. The now popular retro-styled A&W's have returned to Hamilton, with locations near the original sites on Queenston Road and on Upper James, and the return of an all new A&W at the same King Street location as before.

The intense custom car cruising tradition in Hamilton that lasted all through the 1960's and well into the 1970's has faded into history. Restaurant owners retired, locations shut down, and car enthusiasts stopped cruising. During this era, it really was a special time and place, with the situations just right for such an experience to occur. Many of those that participated back then now look back with fond memories of this unique era of Hamilton history.

Photographs courtesy of the following: Milt Houle, Hamilton Historic photos, McMaster University, and the author's collection.

CHAPTER SIX
London

London, Ontario is one of the larger cities within the province of Ontario. Centrally located within an important Southern Ontario manufacturing corridor, London is located about 100 miles east of Windsor, about 90 miles west of Toronto, and about 50 miles from the border town of Sarnia.

In the 1950's, the city's population reached approximately 130,000 citizens. At that time, some of the biggest industries in the city included Imperial Oil, Carlings and Labatt's Breweries, and Club House Foods.

With this many people in one city, it was inevitable that the car culture in London was vibrant. The London Auto Modifiers Canada's oldest hot rod club has roots that go back to 1947. Club members were instrumental in the beginnings of drag racing in the province of Ontario. With the club's help and participation, early era hot rodders enjoyed safe and secure drag race events at Fingal, Kohler, St. Thomas and Port Albert air strips. The members of the London Auto Modifiers were also instrumental in early custom car shows, when they set up the first Canadian Autorama shows in the 1950's. This heritage car club remains an important link in Ontario hot rodding history.

Original club crest for the London Auto Modifiers

With the city in close proximity to St. Thomas Dragway and Grand Bend Dragway, speed shops and hot car garages sprang up all over town during the early 1960's.

Notable shops in London included Kydd Radiator on Hamilton Road, the home of Bill Kydd's "Wills Fargo" altered drag roadster.

Early version of "Will's Fargo" A/Altered beside Kydd Radiator Shop. (left to right) Victor Young, Alex Litt, Bill Kydd Sr., Bill Kydd Jr.

Another racing legend from London was "Ontario George" Gray, who built a series of competitive drag coupes at Jordan Gray Garage on Egerton Street.

George Gray's '33 Willys in 1970

Scott Wilson's dragster launches at St. Thomas Dragway

Other speed shops in the London area included Atchison Machine Shop in York Street, Speed & Sport Specialties on Oak Street, Miller & Gregory on Southcrest Drive, A&K Speed, operated by Lloyd Noxell, out on Hamilton Road, and Competition Motors on Nightingale, operated by Craig Hill and Al Wright.

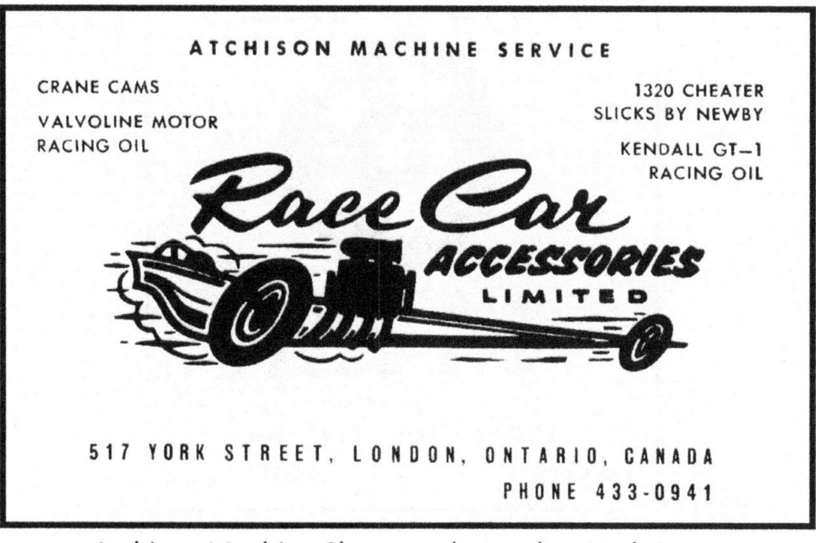

Atchison Machine Shop was located on York Street

Speed & Sport was a small shop on Oak Street

Miller & Gregory's shop was the home of "Well's Wheels"

Lloyd Noxell was manager of A&K Speed Shop

T-bucket street roadster built by Al Wright

Throughout the 1960's, the performance division of several local car dealerships thrived in the competitive "hot street car" market in the city of London. The London-based dealership of Rankin Ford, on the corner of Dundas Street and Highbury, not only grew throughout the decade, but two of their service mechanics became well known for the race car they built within Rankin Ford's service bay. John McIntyre and Ev Rouse worked together on a Ford Falcon that became known as "The Wild Child", setting records at drag strips throughout the province.

Rankin FORD
1365 DUNDAS AT HIGHBURY London East 455-1800
SAVE MORE AT CANADA'S LARGEST RETAILER OF FORD PRODUCTS

Rankin Ford on Dundas at Highbury

Rankin Ford's "Save-A-Lot" car lot

"The Wild Child" Ford Falcon, sponsored by Rankin Ford
The car was raced by mechanics Ev Rouse and John McIntyre

Central
LTD.
CHEV LONDON OLDS

CENTRAL
CHEVROLET
OLDSMOBILE
SERVICE
ENTRANCE
COLEMAN'S

Wayne Huber and Dave Mathers both worked at Central Chevrolet on Fullerton Street, each making their mark in local drag racing circles. Dave Mathers became the tech inspector at St. Thomas Dragway in the mid-1960's, and Wayne Huber's experience as a top notch builder and tuner of race motors helped plenty of local racers reach the winner's circle at championship events.

Pontiac performance vehicles were readily available for purchase at London Motor Products on Richmond Street.

London Motor Products were on Richmond Street

If it was Chrysler muscle cars you were looking for, they could have been acquired at McManus Motors, with a wide selection to choose from within their enormous showroom.

In the early 1950's, the London scene was very laid back. Favourite meeting places for young people centered on several restaurants located in the downtown area, including the Campus Hi-Fi Food Bar, with its close proximity to the University of Western.

Campus Hi-Fi Food Bar on Richmond Street

Other popular meet ups included the Maple Leaf Restaurant at 256 Dundas Street, Pat's Lunch on Oxford Street, and the Peppermint Lounge, a diner that featured a busy dance floor.

Maple Leaf Restaurant was a downtown fav for years

Neon signs outside the Maple Leaf Restaurant

Pat's Lunch on Oxford Street

Peppermint Lounge Dine and Dance

Peppermint Lounge's rockin' jukebox on the dance floor

As the emerging car culture swept over the city, drive-in restaurants catering to the car quickly became the centre of even more activity.

First and foremost was the unique restaurant known as "The Three Little Pigs Pentry" on Wharncliffe Road. Owned and operated by Earl Nichols, the "Pigs" first opened in 1934, and for more than 30 years, the restaurant offered the community a totally unique dining experience.

In its prime during the 1950's, Three Little Pigs Pentry was considered a must-visit for anyone in the London area. Table service inside the restaurant was very popular with families. Car enthusiasts enjoyed the curb service, where tray-wielding car hops brought freshly prepared food directly to your car.

Three Little Pigs Pentry on Wharncliffe Road

Perhaps the most unusually named restaurant anywhere

Car hop curb service and indoor seating at "The Pigs"

Madgwick's DRIVE-IN RESTAURANT

Located across town from Three Little Pigs Pentry, Madgwicks on Dundas Street East offered a more traditional drive-in experience. Their menu including burgers, hot dogs, French fries and milkshakes served up to each customer with traditional car hop service. For the London area car enthusiast, not only was the food superb, but the parking lot easily held more cars than was ever available at "Three Little Pigs Pentry". Another key reason for the restaurant's popularity among London area gearheads was its location out past Crumlin Road on a decidedly more remote "out in the middle of nowhere" section of Dundas Street. The distance from other businesses provided opportunities to show off your hot car's power abilities in front of a large crowd without hassle from the police.

Madgwick's, a classic drive-in restaurant with great food, car hop service, and a parking lot that held more cars than at "The Pigs"

Delicious turkey with dressing, french fries, cole slaw and roll.

89c

Good Food Tastefully Prepared.

Madgwick's — ½ Mile East of Crumlin

Specials every weekend at Madgwick's Drive-In

The first of three London A&W Drive-Ins soon opened on York Street at Burwell, with a parking lot so large, it extended all the way to King Street. Because of its close proximity to the downtown cruising strip, the York Street A&W quickly became a major cruising destination for many London hot rodders.

Car hop Gail Condie serves customers at the York Street A&W

During the early 1960's, London's cruising scene eagerly expanded as more drive-in restaurants opened up throughout the city limits.

A second A&W Drive-In opened in the city at 2061 Dundas Street East, becoming a direct competitor for the clientele of the already established Madgwick's, just down the road.

Car hop curb service at the A&W on Dundas Street East

Further down Wharncliffe from Three Little Pigs Pentry saw the opening of Sol's Square Boy Drive-In, owned and operated by Saul Holiff, the one-time manager of county music superstar Johnny Cash. This popular drive-in was quite the hot spot during the 1960's, filling the parking lot with cars and people on a nightly basis.

Sol's Square Boy Drive-In on Wharncliffe Road

Sol's Square Boy's popular and extensive menu

Customers order meals from a remote ordering system

Owner Saul Holiff works the register during a busy shift

Entrepreneur Saul Holiff had also gained fame for booking live rock and roll shows into the London Arena, often bringing some of these musical stars to his drive-in for a personal appearance and autograph session.

Rock & Roll star Bill Haley with Saul Holiff

Bill Haley and Saul Holiff at Sol's Square Boy Drive-In

SAUL HOLIFF PRESENTS .... IN PERSON

"THE BIG BEAT SHOW"
LONDON ARENA
THURSDAY, APRIL 10, 8:30 P.M.

Major league rock & roll concert, promoted by Saul Holiff

In the early 1960's, Harvey's opened their first location at 160 Wharncliffe Road South, half way between Sol's Square Boy and Three Little Pigs Pentry. In their continuous effort to capitalize on the robust cruising action through the downtown core, Harvey's opened a second drive-in at 590 Dundas.

NOW
2 LOCATIONS TO
SERVE YOU BETTER

Harvey's Drive-in is proud to announce the

GRAND OPENING

OF ANOTHER SPARKLING NEW LOCATION

590 DUNDAS

(At Adelaide)

HARVEY'S

CHARCOAL -BROILED

HAMBURGERS
CHEESEBURGERS
HOT-DOGS

This offer is available at both locations

160 Wharncliffe Rd. S.

590 Dundas St.

PRESENT THIS COUPON AND RECEIVE

FREE FRENCH FRIES

WITH YOUR PURCHASE OF HAMBURGER - CHEESEBURGER OR HOT DOG

A&W Drive-In opens at 426 Springbank Drive in London

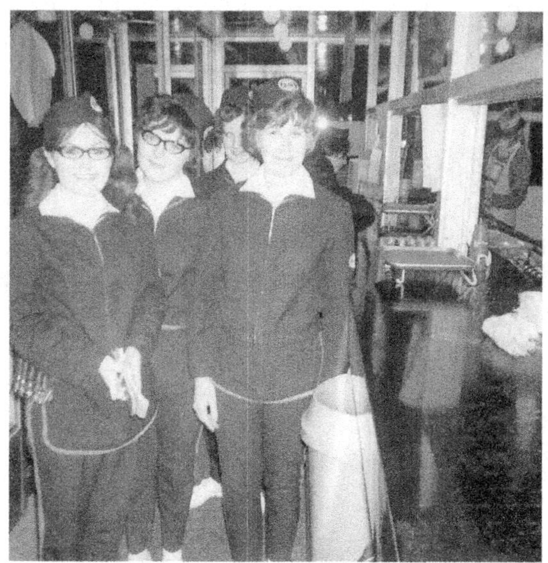

Car hops ready for customers at Springbank A&W

During all eras of the cruising scene in London, it was mandatory to cruise the downtown core on Dundas Street. The stores, the theatres, and the overall general excitement all stemmed from a trip down the strip. Every clever hot rodder in town memorized the approximate show times for each of the major theatres along Dundas Street. Timing is everything, so the key was to find yourself cruising by the Dundas Street exit doors outside both the Century and the Capitol Theatres just as the crowds left the movie house each evening. Hot cars and large crowds on the street made for big time cruising fun.

Cruising on Dundas begins before dark

The nightly parade on Dundas

Cruising Dundas was even more fun after dark

Cruising on York Street was fun even in wet weather

King Street in London

In the 1950's, London's cruising circuit was less defined, with most enthusiasts just discovering the fun associated with this newly found sense of freedom and fun. Generally, most early cruisers started at Three Little Pigs. After meeting up with your buddies, you would turn onto Dundas, drive the entire length of the downtown strip all the way out to Madgwicks. After a time, you would turn around and head back to the "Pigs".

By the early 1960's, the cruising increased as the number of drive-in restaurants were opened in the city. Starting at Sol's Square Boy on Wharncliffe road, you traveled back to the "Pigs" on Wharncliffe, then to the A&W on York Road. After circling the large parking lot, you would find your way to Dundas Street, slowly cruise through the downtown heading towards the A&W at 2061 Dundas Street East, and then out to Madgwicks Drive In. After your mandatory stop at Madgwicks, it was a return trip back down Dundas, with a stop at Harvey's Drive-In at 590 Dundas across from the police station, then off for a return trip to "Pigs" and Sol's, and a stop at the Harvey's at 160 Wharncliffe.

By the 1970's, even though several of the original cruising destinations had closed and faded into history, newer locations opened up, creating a new legacy. The Mr. Sub location opened during this later era, creating an all new meeting place for serious cruisers in London, and the interest of cruising along Dundas was still strong.

London's elaborate cruising route was simply a part of living in a large city with a lot of excellent places to cruise. In later years, some diehards chose one or two locations to frequent, making their cruise route easier to navigate. However, as everyone remembers, there were always those magical warm summer nights that you never wanted the evening or the cruising to end.

Shared memories courtesy of the following: John Chandler, John Stenabaugh, John Willoughby, Mark Rogerson, Stewart Addley, Bonnie Cogan DeSando, Lori Wright, Sandy Lynn, Bill Westgate, Dianne Kehoe Lawrence, Janet Costello Massie, Debbie Peters Cameron, Ted Belbeck, Linda Jean Tupholme, Karen Brown, Victoria Sintzel, Harley Handy, Marilyn Thompson, Pete Bauslaugh, Louise Wolfenden Smithrim, Sally Morritt, David Roper, Shirley Wise, Vonita Lynn, Rosemarie Sillers, Frank Sorrenti, Syd Floyd, Mary Lynn Drzewiecki, Jean Lynn Arthur, Debby Zalizniak, Teri Robertson, Debbie Knowles, Janet Smith, Gail Condie, Jack Edwards, Wayne Stenning, Barbara Hamon, Tim Burgess, Catherine Ormandy, Steve Jackson, Norman Jones, Fred Fuller, Bonnie Grube, Fred Weyerman, Tobie Gosling, Michael Berard Rubini, Trudy Sims, Paul Clubb, Suzanne Couture, Robert Wood, Corrie Woudenberg-Foerster, John Ladd, John Seabrook,

Special thanks to: Bill Kydd, George Gray, Jonathan Holiff, Ed Heal, David MacHay, and Cindy Hartman.

CHAPTER SEVEN
Stratford

You could easily consider this community to be the perfect city to live in. Picturesque and full of charm, Stratford, Ontario is located 93 miles West of Toronto, 160 miles East of Windsor, and 112 miles North West of Niagara Falls, Ontario. Stratford boasts a robust downtown area, with wide streets, beautiful plantings of trees and flowers, and historic buildings all through the core area. Nestled next to the scenic Avon River and Victoria Lake is a winding two-lane roadway through parkland that leads to the Festival Theatre, home of the world renowned Stratford Shakespeare Festival.

In the early 1960's, the city boasted a population of about 21,000 citizens, swelling to double that size during the festival season. The tourist aspect of town brought droves of shoppers and festival goers into the city, welcomed by all residents and shop owners throughout the community. As the famous festival began to draw new people into the area, a population growth spike took hold, spurred on by the natural charm and quality of life within the city of Stratford. For those who grew up during the 1950's and '60's, life in Stratford had its benefits as well.

CJCS radio in Stratford

During the late 1950's and throughout the 1960's, there was plenty of activities for the burgeoning Stratford youth culture. Opportunities for the era's teenagers ranged from roller skating at the Coliseum, and dances to live bands at Club 42 on Ontario Street.

Roller skating and dances at the Coliseum

New! New!!

Teen "Go-Go" Dance

To the Pharaos

8:30 – 11:30 50¢ admission

UPSTAIRS – COLISEUM

Supervised by Rotary Members

SAT.NITE

The Return of the

BEDTIME STORY

ADVANCE TICKETS – 1.25
Club 42 – Thurs., Fri. & Sat. 3 – 5 p.m.
At The Door – 1.50

NEXT SAT. NITE

THE MAGIC CYCLE

Dances at Club 42

Club 42

This Thurs. Sept. 7th
THE GUESS WHO

Saturday, Sept. 9th
THE LUV-LITES
& THE TIARAS

42 Wellington, Stratford, Ont.

Big time entertainment at Club 42

Out at the corner of Lorne Avenue and Downie Streets beckoned the Stratford Drive-In Theatre, and for decades, this was an extremely popular destination on a warm summer evening.

Several downtown restaurants became natural places for friends to meet up, share some great food, and to venture out from to some other fun activities. Noteworthy in this category during the earliest days of the era include Scrim's Booth, a tiny diner at the corner of Huron and Douglas, serving freshly prepared burgers and fries.

Located in the heart of the downtown core was Ellam's Restaurant, a legendary local eatery best remembered for Cherry Cokes and a heaping plate of fresh cut fries.

Another summertime Stratford destination has been a mandatory trip to the Erie Drive-In, located at 634 Erie Street. Famous for their ice cream and foot-long hot dogs, the Erie Drive-In was always a fun stop for a treat, especially before or after a visit to the Stratford Drive-In, a short 6 blocks away.

Erie Drive-In

As any local gear head can tell you, Stratford has also had a strong reputation and long history of being a "hot car" town. Custom car and hot rod enthusiasts clearly took advantage of the wide, busy downtown sections of Ontario, Erie, Downie, and Huron Streets to conduct some serious cruising.

Ontario Street, Stratford's main drag.
Noted local 1955 Chevy parked on the left

Wayne Yundt's "Apache" 1932 Ford show & street coupe

Vince Gratton's street driven 1935 Ford coupe

Hishon Brother's C/Gas 1939 Willy's drag coupe

Jack Hyde's B/Stock Chevrolet race car

Two legendary drive-in restaurants were located on either end of town, guiding Stratford's cruising enthusiasts into a natural flow through the downtown core. Located at 1010 Ontario Street was The Thunderbird, a typical 1960's era drive-in restaurant that featured a standard menu of hamburgers, hot dogs, onion rings and French fries, served curbside from friendly car hops. After ownership changes, the restaurant was rechristened the Jolly Buccaneer, remaining a very popular drive-in throughout the 1960's and into the 1970's.

Thunderbird Drive-In, renamed the Jolly Buccaneer

JOLLY BUCCANEER
Drive-In Restaurant

1010 Ontario
Stratford, Ontario

271-2300

Across town, the A&W Drive-in opened along Huron Street, back in 1960. As any car enthusiast is quick to point out, a need to find out what cars are out cruising that night, and who else may be hanging around at either place on any given evening brings on the need to cruise through the downtown area on a regular basis.

Stratford's A&W on Huron Street opened in 1960

A&W on Huron, with Loblaws just down the street

The natural cruise route kickoff in Stratford was to meet your buddies at the A&W on Huron. More than likely, most visitors ordered a Teenburger, a side order of "Coney Fries" and a frosted mug of root beer. After chatting with your friends and checking out the cars in the parking lot, it was time to hit the street.

Before leaving the parking lot, it was a right of passage to do a quick burn out up against the parking lot's last speed bump near the road. After the smoke cleared, you would turn right onto Huron Street and venture down the road for about 6 blocks, heading over the bridge and turning right onto Erie Street. After a quick trip through the parking lot at the Erie Drive-In, turn back onto Erie, then left onto Lorne Avenue, taking you towards the Stratford Drive-In, at the corner of Lorne and Downie. Make a left onto Downie and head north until you reach Ontario Street.

The downtown beckons, as stores and businesses were lit up with neon signs, and the streets are filled with young people enjoying a warm summer night heightened by a sense of fun and excitement. With on-street parking on both sides, Ontario Street was busy and usually filled with cars. This stretch of the main drag has always been a great place to drive your car, cruising low and slow along Ontario Street for about two miles, on your way to the Thunderbird, a drive-in restaurant at 1010 Ontario Street. After arriving at the T-Bird, you would check out the cars and people that were in the parking lot, while munching down on some tasty food. Years later, the restaurant changed ownership and was then renamed The Jolly Buccaneer.

Eager to hit the streets to continue their cruising journey, many of the dedicated car fraternity would leave the Thunderbird and head back downtown to see who had congregated along the strip before returning back to the A&W on Huron Street.

Another popular additional diversion in Stratford's cruising circuit included a journey along Lakeside Drive. This picturesque tranquil setting features Lake Victoria on one side, and beautifully maintained parkland surrounding the Stratford Festival Theatre on the other side. For many of the Stratford cruising enthusiasts, this side journey is an endeavor that remains popular to this day.

Cruising through the park along Lakeside Drive

While there were many car devotees that cruised along the streets of downtown Stratford, there also was a parallel group of serious street race fanatics that would also gather together at the A&W on a regular basis.

As the evening sky grew darker and the hour grew closer to midnight, a deliberately slow procession of hot cars would leave the A&W parking lot, heading single file towards several nearby Stratford back streets.

Moving gingerly along Mornington Street, these cars headed out of town in the general direction of the Stratford Municipal Airport. The destination of these drivers was Perth Line 43, known locally as Amulree Road.

This stretch of road directly past the airport property is a perfectly flat straightaway with no side roads for the first several miles. With a wood lot on the left, the far reaches of the airport property on the right, and no houses anywhere nearby, this road is more than perfectly suited for some serious nighttime action. This unintentional back road speedway has been a popular street racing hotspot for several generations.

Perth Line 43 also known as Amulree Road

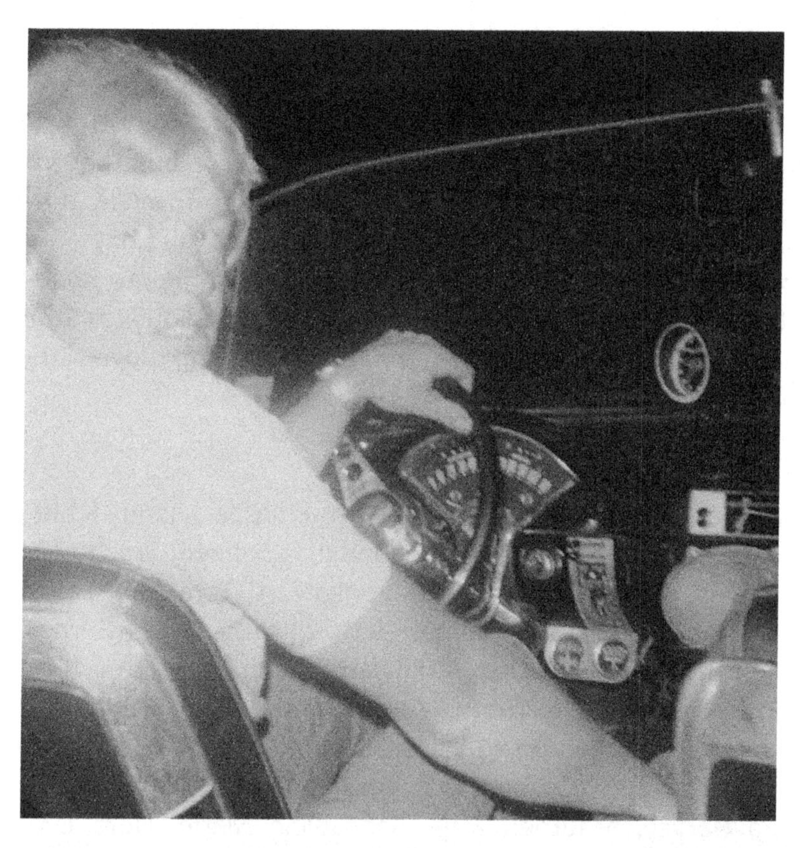

Late night racing out on Amulree Road in the 1970's

Today, Stratford remains a charming city with lots of character and appeal. Hot cars are still in abundance all through the community, and the legacy of Stratford's early car culture remains strong. The Jolly Buccaneer and the A&W are gone today, but the cruising tradition along Ontario Street and the journey through the park next to the Festival Theatre continues to this day. While unadvertised showdowns still occur along the Amulree Road strip on the occasional late summer evening, all car activities in Stratford are certainly paired down from what they were like over 50 years ago.

Memories shared by the following: Doug Jasper, Randy Smith, Ted Kovacs, Dave Burnett, Wilf Sukowski, Kathleen Trachsel, Dave Schulthies, Phyllis Humphrey, Dave Dotzert, Tom Rau, Lew Pfaff, Randy Yielding, Stave Rome, Jeff Myles, Terry Gerber, Ed Mulholland, Tom Sylvester, Al Edwards, John Lichti, Larry Douglas, Dennis Smith, Corrie Thorn, Karen Smith, Brad Brodhagen, Joe Hishon, David Drane, David Taylor, Bev and George Edwards, Nancy Glaab, Mary Payne, Debra Davidge, Patti Farrell, Sandra Voison, Debra Harvey, Maureen Hopf, Jacqueline Marie, Nora E. Swan, Dennis Manktelow, Paula Walsh Hazen.

Special thank you to Gary Dale, Vince Gratton, Bruce Hislop, Susan Wigan, Brent Harvey, and all of the enthusiastic supporters at the "If you grew up in Stratford" Facebook group.

CHAPTER EIGHT
Welland

Downtown Welland at night

Welland, Ontario is a small city located smack dab in the middle of the Niagara Peninsula, 15 miles from the city of St. Catharines, and 16 miles from Niagara Falls, Ontario. With the city cut in half by the Welland Canal Waterway system, it has developed into its own unique community, unlike any other in the region.

By the 1950's, Welland was home to about 30,000 residents, with a large and diverse population of young people, and becoming a unique and popular cruising destination over the years.

Several local hot rod car clubs had formed in and around Welland, including the Road Beavers Car Club in 1958, as well as the nearby Fonthill Road Lions, the Pacers Car Club in Port Colbourne, and the Shafters Hot Rod Club in Niagara Falls. Each member of these car clubs shared a goal of bringing responsibility and respectability to the hot rod hobby in the minds of citizens throughout the city, as well as the Welland police.

Welland-area roadster was seen on the streets and at winter shows

Hot rod roadsters were popular in Welland

Young people throughout the 1950's and 1960's spent their time attending dances, and enjoying roller skating at the Welland Arena, a large hall that was constantly booked with activities for young and old. As soon as the hockey season was finished in the spring, this facility was also the site used for indoor custom car shows over the years.

CHOW radio's mammoth Hi-Fi dance at the Welland Arena

Roller Skating
TUESDAY

Afternoon—1:30-4

Children 10c

Evening club skating

7:30-9 Public skating

9-11

Welland-Crowland Arena

Roller skating at the Welland Arena

2ND CAR ANNUAL

WELLAND AUTORAMA

JUNE 9, 10, 11

To be held in the **WELLAND ARENA** which gives adequate show room and seating room for the ladies.

THIS YEAR'S SHOW WILL FEATURE

★ **HOT RODS** ★ **DRAGSTERS**

★ **CUSTOMS** ★ **MODIFIED SPORTS CARS**

Sponsored by three Welland area hot rod clubs

Welland Autorama custom car show

Pete White with his award winning hot rod at Welland Autorama

COOPE'S
SHELL SERVICE

- GENERAL REPAIRS
- ROAD SERVICE
- CAR WASHING
- BATTERIES

FREE PICK UP & DELIVERY

RE 2-3403

503 NIAGARA N (AT THOROLD RD.)
COOPE'S SERVICE STATION

Doug Coope & John Bisson on a lunch break between service jobs

BALON'S
WHITE ROSE

SERV STN

24 HR.
TOWING

Licensed Mechanic
Tune-Up & Repairs

MUFFLERS & TAIL-PIPES INSTALLED

RE 2-6713

937 MAIN E

AFTER HOURS CALL RE 5-5935

STAGER'S
SUNOCO SERVICE STATION

PICK UP & DELIVERY
OPEN 7 A.M. - 11 P.M.

RE 2-5501
WELLAND JUNCTION

Richards
speed & wheel centre
"The One Stop Speed Shop"

NEW PARTS
114 DIVISION
WELLAND
735-8230

NEW & USED PARTS
30 ST PAUL ST
ST CATHARINES **684-3778**

SERVICE
39 PELHAM RD
ST CATHARINES **688-2651**

Sponsored race car in front of Lauro's Garage

Triangle Garage on Niagara Street

Throughout the 1950's, many of Welland's youthful population would gather at one or more of the local restaurants that were open in the downtown area. Popular diners in Welland included the Bright Spot on King Street, and Tully's Diner located at 20 Cross Street.

BRIGHT SPOT

RESTAURANT

GEORGE TRENT

607 King St., WELLAND

Phone 9092

George Trent's Bright Spot on King Street

Tully's Diner on Cross Street

The minute that the A&W Drive-In opened up at 123 Riverside Drive, many serious Welland-area car aficionados finally had a proper place to meet. This location quickly became the city's premier cruising destination, featuring the hottest cars and the biggest crowds in town. On a summer evening, parking in the lot became a serious challenge, with hot rods and custom cars coming and going throughout the evening.

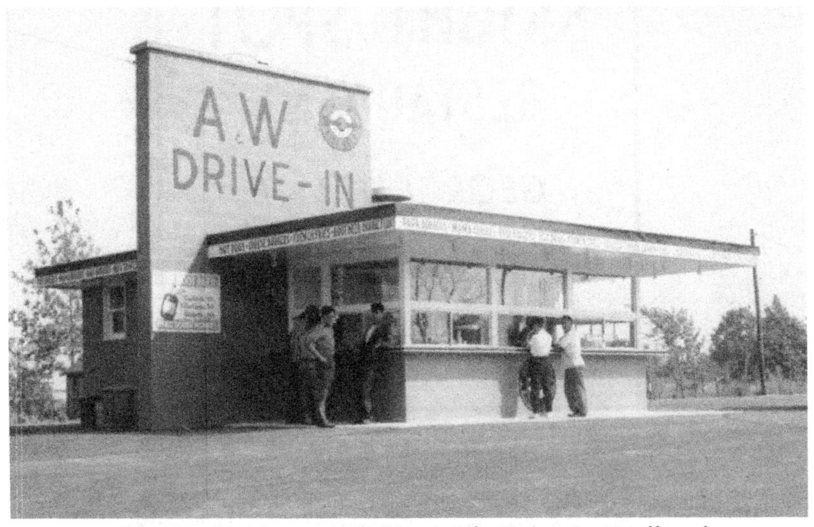

A&W Drive-In at 123 Riverside Drive in Welland

During the 1960's, Welland's downtown area was a natural draw for extracurricular activities for car enthusiasts. Cruising had its unique areas as well, developing naturally along East Main, the central commercial street in town. Main becomes a one-way street at Ross, as it continues along through the downtown area. Turning left on King and another left onto Division Street takes you along that commercial strip for about 5 blocks as the street eventually bends upward to meet up with Main Street again. This was the earliest downtown cruising pattern for most Welland enthusiasts.

Constant traffic along East Main in downtown Welland

For those wishing to pursue their need for speed, a side trip off the main drag began with a hard left onto King Street which runs along parallel to the canal, as the road pointed toward the outer reaches of the city limit. After another hard left onto Ontario Street, a long stretch of straight pavement greeted these Welland speed freaks.

This natural straightaway became a proving ground for many of Welland's local high performance car enthusiasts in town. The lack of houses or problematic cross roads for several blocks along Ontario Street made for a perfect short sprint drag strip.

Ontario Road, a mostly deserted strip on the edge of town

After a quick trip down Ontario Road, it was a short drive along Southworth Street. This northbound thoroughfare suddenly turns into Crowland Avenue after crossing Lincoln Street, which takes you back to East Main Street, Welland's main cruising strip.

By the late 1960's, A&W closed its original location on Riverside Drive after franchise operators built a brand new Drive-In at the corner of East Main and Scholfield, along Welland's busy main drag. After several quality passes down Main Street and along Division Street, many hot cars ended up in the parking lot at the A&W on East Main for some food, soft drinks, and a long rap session with car friends that had gathered at this popular cruising destination.

A&W Drive-In on East Main at Scholfield

Two-seater sports cars at A&W meant summertime fun

Nighttime cruising fun in downtown Welland

The cruising tradition in Welland that had started in the early 1950's had begun to fade by the late 1970's. When the A&W Drive-In on East Main closed down in 1985, it spelled the end of a fun era for a lot of hot rod enthusiasts in the city of Welland.

Shared memories by the following: Jim Bray, Jeanette Mittlestead, Cathy Ristine Allaster, Jim Ryan, Dennis Dutkus, Pat Durand, Jeanine Fortier, John Blackwell, Bradley Ulch, and members of the "If you grew up in Welland" Facebook group.

Photos from the collections of Jim Ryan, Milt Houle, Sophie Woch, Mark Vasco, and Tim Sykes.

CHAPTER 9
Woodstock

Dundas Street in downtown Woodstock

Centrally located in the middle of Southwestern Ontario is the picturesque community of Woodstock, Ontario, a city with plenty of small town charm. Back in 1960, just over twenty thousand citizens called Woodstock their home. Access off the mighty 401 corridor along Oxford, this stretch of Highway 2 becomes Dundas Street, which is the 2 mile business section of Main Street through the central section of town.

During the early 1960's, Dundas Street became the focus of most teenage motor fanatics in the region as the most popular place to cruise in the city. At each end of the strip were two favourite destinations that became the anchor for most cruising activities.

At the east end of Dundas Street was The Skooba Drive-In Restaurant. At the west end was The Chuck Wagon Drive-In. In between these two local landmarks was a strip of busy and prosperous downtown store fronts, all eager to meet the needs of their customers, young and old.

The New SKOOBA DRIVE-IN RESTAURANT

Dundas St. E. - WOODSTOCK

Built in the late 1950's, the Skooba Drive-In was a very popular destination throughout the 1960's. Located at 943 Dundas Street East, a large neon sign located near the street lit up the nighttime sky, directing hungry patrons towards the main parking lot for the restaurant. Patrons either ate their food in their cars or at the various picnic tables located near the parking lot. Owned and operated by Jim Stansfield and Bob Hewitt, the Skooba Drive-In became so popular that a few short years after opening, it was expanded to double its original size.

Newly renovated Skooba Drive-In

At nightfall, The Skooba was a wonderland of sight and sound

Situated at 7 Ingersoll Road, just off of the Dundas strip on the west end of town is the Chuck Wagon Drive-In. This quaint eatery, in business for more than 8 decades, was originally operated as Danny's Lunch.

Hamburgs & Hot Dogs at

DANNY'S LUNCH

Are Dee - Licious

WE SPECIALIZE IN TAKE OUT ORDERS

PHONE 2777J

INGERSOLL RD. & DUNDAS ST.

With a change of name and ownership in the 1960's, The Chuck Wagon Drive-In has endured many years as a local favourite. Even with a gravel parking lot, it remains a popular cruising destination and the natural turn-round area for local cruising enthusiasts.

The Chuck Wagon Drive-In on Ingersoll Road

Now Open
Chuck Wagon Drive In
CURB SERVICE • COMPLETE FOUNTAIN SERVICE
DELICIOUS SANDWICHES • HOURS: 1 P. M. to 1 A. M.
Our
Chuck Wagon
Special!
New and Different
Barbecued Hamburgers
20¢

20 cent hamburgers at the Chuck Wagon Drive-In

While Woodstock had several thriving car clubs in town, such as the Golden Falcons and the Hi-Risers, it was the draw of Woodstock's Dundas Street cruising strip that often brought members of the Road Rebels Car Club into town from nearby Norwich, Ontario.

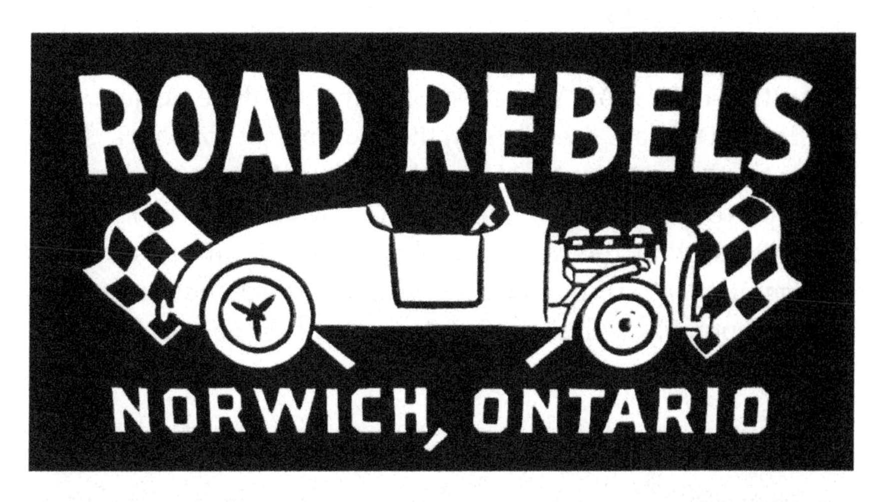

Members of the Norwich Road Rebels

With most car enthusiasts in the various communities throughout Ontario that participated in the cruising tradition, the popular terms referred to the practice as "Cruising Main Street" or "Cruising the Drag". Within the city of Woodstock, the cruising term used here was "Cruisin' the Dig".

During the 1960's, A&W opened one of their drive-ins just across and down Dundas Street from the Skooba, becoming a serious threat to the popularity of the longtime Woodstock landmark. Many patrons began to divide their loyalty between the two competitors, with the Skooba feeling a decline in sales after the opening of A&W. Throughout the decade though, both restaurants remained popular with the car enthusiasts of Woodstock.

A&W Drive-In on Dundas Street in Woodstock

Because of the fact that the main drag was only a relatively short 2 mile stretch, many young pedestrians that were not in cars would either window shop along the business section or simply take up residence on a downtown bench and watch the action drift by.

1957 Chevy out Cruisin' the Dig

Kevin Barlow's 1971 Chevelle

Carloads of young people in cars would continuously drive up and down Dundas Street on a warm summer evening in a seemingly endless parade.

Terry Easby's Beaumont

Gary Perry's 1969 Fairlaine

Scott Robinson's 1967 Mustang

More than a few cruising enthusiasts would regularly pull off of Dundas into the expansive downtown parking lot in front of Towers Department Store. The lineup of cars in the parking lot facing Dundas varied throughout the evening, as these participants would sit and watch the cars on Dundas go by before rejoining the action.

Enormous parking lot at Towers Plaza on Dundas

Cuda and Camaro owners at Towers watch the action on Dundas

In the middle of the action on Dundas Street

Hot rods and muscle cars out on Dundas in Woodstock

The cruising scene in Woodstock lasted much longer than most communities on Ontario. As the 1960's turned in the 1970's and '80's, the cruising adapted to the changes as well. When many other communities throughout Ontario lost interest in cruising, the scene in Woodstock continued with an amazingly vibrant street racing effort. Straight stretches of back roads surrounding the outskirts of town were scouted and found by eager gearheads. These seldom used sections of straight pavement were selected because of their lack of dangerous cross roads, or nearby houses with hidden driveways. Having no neighbours in the immediate area means less of a worry about noise complaints or an unexpected appearance from the local police. These noted strips then were given individual "code" names, providing an interesting variety of local drag strips perfectly suited for the performance minded enthusiasts in the Woodstock area.

Woodstock's well organized secret racing action

Several different locations were used in efforts to avoid detection

Wild street racing activities on little used roads just outside of town

Today, Woodstock continues to be a popular cruising destination, even in the 21st century. Much of the downtown core remains very similar to the way it was during the early cruising days, back in the 1950's and all through the '60's. Even though many of the original destinations are long gone, there is still a cruising heritage that continues to be enjoyed in the city.

Shared memories courtesy of the following: Scott Robinson, Jeff Brydges, Rob Wadel, Glen Tovey, Carl Adams, Bob Deadman, Kevin Barlow, JD Robinson, Larry McGee, Greg Barnes, Dave Keeping, Josephine Lonsberry, Wayne Skillings, Gail Bell Kellar, Nancy McCabe, Judi Hill McLeod, Steve Lorch, Jonny Bee, Gordon Worsnop, Kelly Sherman, John Burman, Bill Beavin, Terry Stitts, Linda Wells, Diana Maginnis-Noyce, JJ Stansfield, Debi Dalgarno, Gloria Ludington, Cheryl Hastie, Patrick Muttart, Jim Cowan, Daniel Fredrick Frank, Dianne Coomber, Susan Wilson, Pat Lapier, Margaret Edwards, Dale Totten, Pat McDonald.

Special thanks to Ken Roberts for photos and memories, as well as members of the "Woodstock Car Scene" Facebook Page, and members of the "You Know You Grew Up in Woodstock" Facebook Page.

About the Author

For more than 30 years, author Tim Sykes has been writing about the history of Canadian rods & customs, drag racing, and cruising.

His work has appeared in the pages of hot rod magazines and automotive publications in both Canada and the United States.

He has written 5 other history books that are available at the **pitsideshop.com** website.

Tim Sykes and his wife Jill live in the beautiful and historic West Galt "gaslight" district of Cambridge, Ontario, Canada.

Made in the USA
Monee, IL
13 September 2021